J. M. (James Monroe) Buckley

Christian Science and Other Superstitions

J. M. (James Monroe) Buckley

Christian Science and Other Superstitions

ISBN/EAN: 9783744665230

Printed in Europe, USA, Canada, Australia, Japan

Cover: Foto ©Lupo / pixelio.de

More available books at **www.hansebooks.com**

CHRISTIAN SCIENCE
AND OTHER SUPERSTITIONS

BEING SELECTED CHAPTERS FROM
"FAITH-HEALING, CHRISTIAN SCIENCE,
AND KINDRED PHENOMENA"

BY
J. M. BUCKLEY, LL.D.

NEW YORK
THE CENTURY CO.
1899

Copyright, 1886, 1887, 1888, 1889, 1892, 1899, by
THE CENTURY CO.

THE DE VINNE PRESS.

EXPLANATORY NOTE

THE essays herein contained were printed in the "Century Magazine": that on Faith Healing in June, 1886, and that on Christian Science in July of the following year. Afterward these, with several others which treated Dreams, Nightmare, Somnambulism, Presentiments, Visions, Apparitions, Astrology, Divination, and Witchcraft, were published by the Century Company in a volume entitled "Faith Healing, Christian Science, and Kindred Phenomena," which has had a wide circulation. They excited much discussion, but neither the authenticity of any fact nor the accuracy of any quotation has been impeached.

In the intervening time the author has given close attention to the moral, scientific, and legal phases of the subject, some of the results of which may be found in the Supplementary Paper prepared expressly for this publication.

Faith Healing and Christian Science are not, as many seem to think, "much the same thing." Faith Healers and Christian Scientists agree in rejecting all medical treatment, but in scarcely anything else. Faith Healers acknowledge the existence of diseased conditions and also the action of remedies; Christian Scientists deny both, affirming that the body, disease, the influence of medicine, and death are "delusions of mortal mind." Faith Healers believe sickness to be the "work of the devil"; Christian Scientists consider that theory a delusion. Faith Healers pray to God—whom they believe to be a person who sent His Son into the world to destroy the works of the devil—to remove disease, and they believe He will do this if, renouncing all dependence on medicine, they exercise faith in Him alone; Christian Sci-

EXPLANATORY NOTE

entists deny the personality of God and do not believe in prayer in the sense of asking God to do anything whatever. Faith Healers assert that Christian Science is a baneful heresy; Christian Scientists consider Faith Healers ignorant of the true meaning of Scripture and grossly superstitious.

The explanation of such recoveries, real and spurious, as are experienced by the respective votaries of these beliefs is fully treated in the article on Faith Healing. Minor variations resulting from their different methods of talking to the sick are accounted for in the article on Christian Science.

CONTENTS

I

FAITH-HEALING

	PAGE
THE FACTS	3
TESTIMONY TO PARTICULARS	6
EXPLANATION OF THE FACTS	14
INDUCTIONS	37
THE MIRACLES OF CHRIST AND HIS APOSTLES	38
CLAIMS OF "CHRISTIAN FAITH-HEALERS," TECHNICALLY SO CALLED, EFFECTUALLY DISCREDITED	41
THE CHRISTIAN DOCTRINE OF ANSWER TO PRAYER	43
DEFENSE OF FAITH-HEALERS EXAMINED	46
ERRORS IN MENTAL PHYSIOLOGY	50
A "MISSING LINK"	52
EVILS OF THIS SUPERSTITION	55
SUPPOSED DIFFICULTIES	60

II

"CHRISTIAN SCIENCE" AND "MIND CURE"

THEORY	69
PRACTICE	77
SPECIMEN TREATMENTS	83
MIND CURERS *versus* FAITH-HEALERS, MESMERISTS, ETC.	87
TESTS OF THE THEORY	89
EXPLANATION OF THEIR ALLEGED SUCCESS	101

III

SUPPLEMENTARY PAPER

	PAGE
RECENT FAILURES OF CHRISTIAN SCIENCE AND FAITH HEALING	119
CONTRAST BETWEEN THE FAILURES AND SUCCESSES OF FAITH HEALING AND CHRISTIAN SCIENCE AND THOSE OF PHYSICIANS	120
IMPORTANT FACTS CONCERNING ALL SICKNESSES	122
THE RELATION OF THE PRACTICE OF CHRISTIAN SCIENCE AND FAITH HEALING TO CIVIL LAW	125

CHRISTIAN SCIENCE
AND OTHER SUPERSTITIONS

FAITH-HEALING

IN 1849 I first saw performances in "animal magnetism." A "professor," of fluency, fine appearance, and marked self-possession, lectured with illustrations; feeble men after being "magnetized" became strong, and persons ordinarily reticent spoke eloquently on subjects suggested by the audience. Great excitement arose, and the attention of medical men was attracted to the curative powers of "magnetism." A dentist, who was also a physician, acquired the art, and a paralytic when under "the influence" moved an arm long useless. Persons whose teeth were extracted felt no pain during the operation.

Some years afterward, at boarding-school, a young man who was very devout occupied a room with me. A revival in town extended to the school, and the young man was brought from a meeting in a "trance" and placed upon the bed. He was unconscious for some hours; his limbs were rigid, and it was possible to lift him by the head and feet without his body yielding in the least degree; nor could the strongest man bend his arms. At length he opened his eyes, uttered pious ejaculations, and relapsed; this recurred at irregular intervals. By one o'clock in the morning he had resumed his natural state. Feeling that he had been the subject of an unusual manifestation of the favor of God, he was very happy for some days. Similar seizures occurred to him during his stay at the institution, whenever religious meetings were unusually fervent.

In 1856, while in college, I first saw the phenomena of spiritualism as displayed by a "trance medium" and "inspirational speaker." Soon afterward I visited the Perfectionist community established by John H. Noyes, where the cure of disease without medicine and the possibility of escaping death were expounded.

In 1857 I found certain "Millerites" or "Adventists" in the interior of Connecticut who claimed power to heal by prayer and without medicine, and—if they could attain sufficient faith—to raise the dead. This they attempted in the case of a young woman who had died of fever, and continued in prayer for her until decomposition compelled the civil authorities to interfere. This case has been paralleled several times recently. Trances were also common among the Millerites at their camp-meetings, as they had been among the early Methodists, Congregationalists in the time of Jonathan Edwards, and certain Presbyterians and Baptists in the early part of this century in the West and South.

In 1859 the famous Dr. Newton arrived in Boston on one of his periodical visits, causing an extraordinary sensation. The lame who visited him leaped for joy, and left their crutches when they departed; in some instances blindness was cured; several chronic cases were relieved, and astonishing results reported confounding ordinary practitioners, and puzzling one or two medical men of national reputation. I made Dr. Newton's acquaintance, and conversed with him at length and with entire freedom. His disciples became numerous; and "healing mediums" and physicians who cure by "laying on of hands" still exist, increasing rather than diminishing in number.

The circumstance of meeting a person who had been in the habit of going into trances in religious meetings, was an easy subject for "mesmerizers," had been cured by a "healer," and finally became a spiritualist and "trance medium," suggested the question whether there might not be a natural susceptibility acted upon by a general law. Nothing which could shed light upon this problem has been knowingly neglected by the writer during the past thirty years.

Two root questions arise concerning the phenomena; they are the inquiries which lie at the foundation of all knowledge: What are the facts, and how may they be explained?

THE FACTS

THE career of Prince Hohenlohe, Roman Catholic Bishop of Sardica, is as well authenticated as any fact in history. Dr. Tuke, in his thoroughly scientific work on the "Influence of the Mind upon the Body," admits his cures as facts. The Prince, who was born in 1794, in Waldenburg, was of high position and broad education, having studied at several universities. When twenty-six years of age, he met a peasant who had performed several astonishing cures, "and from him caught the enthusiasm which he subsequently manifested in healing the sick." I quote two cases on the authority of Professor Onymus of the University of Würtzburg. "Captain Ruthlein, an old gentleman of Thundorf, 70 years of age, who had long been pronounced incurable of paralysis which kept his hand clinched, and who had not left his room for many years, was perfectly cured.

Eight days after his cure he paid me a visit, rejoicing in the happiness of being able to walk freely. . . . A student of Burglauer, near Murmerstadt, had lost for two years the use of his legs; and though he was only partially relieved by the first and second prayer of the Prince, at the third he found himself perfectly well."

Father Mathew was very successful in relieving the sick; after his death multitudes visited his tomb, and of these many were helped and left their crutches there.

In all parts of Roman Catholic countries, and in the Greek churches of Russia, great stacks of crutches, canes, and splints may be seen, which have been left by those who, as Dr. Tuke says, "there is no reason to doubt, have been cured and relieved of contracted joints by the prayers offered at some shrine, or by the supposed efficacy of their relics." Similar results have been seen in Montreal, Canada, within a few years, at solemnities connected with the deaths of certain bishops, one of whom had performed many cures through a long career.

It cannot be denied that many cures occurred at Knock Chapel in Ireland; and also at Lourdes in France, whose fame "is entirely associated with the grotto of Massavielle, where the Virgin Mary is believed, in the Catholic world, to have revealed herself repeatedly to a peasant girl in 1858." This place is resorted to by multitudes of pilgrims from all parts of the world, whose gifts have rendered possible the building of a large church above the grotto, "consecrated in 1876 in the presence of thirty-five cardinals and other high ecclesiastical dignitaries." The gifts have been made by devotees, many of whom claim to have been cured of ailments that defied medical treatment; besides, a large trade is carried on in the water, which is distributed to all parts of the world. I stood by the fountain for hours observing the pilgrims drinking and filling their bottles. A flask which was filled for me has stood on my mantel for several years, and I am bound to say that no serious illness has occurred in the family during that time. Many recoveries follow its use.

Nor is there any reason to doubt that Joseph Gassner, a Catholic priest in Swabia, effected many cures.

Turning from the Roman Catholic and Greek churches to Protestantism, five or six names are conspicuous in connection with the production of cures without the use of medicine, and in answer to prayer.

Dorothea Trudel, a woman living at Manheim, long had an establishment there. Marvelous tales have been told of the cures, some of which have been thoroughly authenticated.

Another name widely known is that of the late Rev. W. E. Boardman, with whom I was acquainted for many years. He had an establishment in the north of London which is designated "Bethshan," and has created quite a sensation. There hundreds of remarkable cures are claimed of cancer, paralysis, advanced consumption, chronic rheumatism, and lameness; and the usual trophies in the shape of canes, crutches, etc., are left behind. They will not allow the place to be called a *hospital*, but the "Nursery of Faith." Their usual mode is to anoint the sufferer with oil and then pray; though considerable variety in method is practised apparently to stimulate faith. They profess to effect many cures by correspondence, and assert that the healing virtues claimed for French and Irish relics by Roman Catholics are not to be compared with those exercised in answer to their prayers.

Dr. Charles Cullis, of Boston, recently deceased, was long noted in connection with healing diseases by faith and prayer, and among his followers has given Old Orchard, Maine, a reputation as great as the grotto at Lourdes has among Catholics.

The Rev. Mr. Simpson, formerly a Presbyterian minister, and now an Independent in the city of New York, has also become prominent, and there can be no doubt of the improvement in health of many of the persons for whom he has prayed. His devotees have enabled him to open a house here to which various persons, among them some ministers, resort when ill.

Mrs. Mix, a colored woman living in the State of Connecticut, had great fame; having been the instrument of the cure of persons who have devoted themselves to faith-healing, attending conventions, writing books, etc. Her death was bewailed by many respectable persons, without distinction of creed, sex, age, or color, who believed that they had been cured through her prayers.

One of the elements of the notoriety of George O. Barnes, the "Mountain Evangelist," of Kentucky, was his oft-announced power to heal.

Having admitted in general that real cures of real diseases are often made, it is necessary to consider more closely the subject of testimony.

TESTIMONY TO PARTICULARS

ALL honest and rational persons are competent to testify whether they feel sick, and whether they seem better, or believe themselves to have entirely recovered after being prayed for and anointed by Boardman, Simpson, or Cullis; but their testimony as to what disease they had, or whether they are entirely cured, is a different matter, and to have value must be scrutinized in every case by competent judges.

In general, diseases are internal or external. It is clear that no individual can know positively the nature of any *internal* disease that he has. The diagnosis of the most skilful physicians may be in error. Post-mortems in celebrated cases have often shown that there had been an entire misunderstanding of the malady. Hysteria can simulate every known complaint: paralysis, heart-disease, and the worst forms of fever and ague. Hypochondria, to which intelligent and highly educated persons of sedentary habits brooding over their sensations are liable, especially if they are accustomed to read medical works and accounts of diseases and of their treatment, will do the same. Dyspepsia has various forms, and indigestion can produce symptoms of organic heart-disease, while diseases of the liver have often been mistaken by eminent physicians for pulmonary consumption. Especially in women do the troubles to which they are most subject give rise to hysteria, in which condition they may firmly believe that they are afflicted with disease of the spine, of the heart, or indeed of all the organs. I heard an intelligent woman "testify" that she had "heart-disease, irritation of the spinal cord, and Bright's disease of the kidneys, and had suffered from them all for *ten years.*" She certainly had some symptoms of all of them. Within eight years a "regular" physician died, the cause, as he supposed on the authority of several examinations, being consumption. A post-mortem showed his lungs sound, and his death to have been caused by diseases the result of the enormous quantities of food and stimulants he had taken to "fight off consumption." The object of these observations is simply to show that testimony that a person has been cured reflects no light upon the problem as to what he or she was cured of, if it was claimed to be an *internal* disease. The solemn assertion of a responsible person that he was cured of heart-disease, can prove only that the symptoms of what he thought was heart-disease have disappeared.

Also, in any state not accompanied with acute pain, testimony to an immediate cure is of no value unless the disease be of an external character and actually disappears before the eye of the witness. All other cures must have the test of time; hence testimony given on the spot, at the grave of Father Mathew, or at Lourdes, or at the camp-meeting at Old Orchard, or in the Tabernacle of Mr. Simpson, can prove merely that then and there the witness was not conscious of pain or weakness, or of the symptoms of the disease which he believed he had.

The foregoing observations relate to internal diseases, but it is by no means easy to determine what an *external* disease is. Tumors are often mistaken for cancers, and cancers are of different species— some incurable by any means known to the medical profession, others curable. It is by these differences that quack cancer-doctors thrive. When the patient has anything resembling cancer, they promptly apply some salve, and if the patient recovers he signs a certificate saying that he was cured of a cancer of a most terrible character which would have been fatal in three months or six weeks; or when the *quack himself writes the certificate for the patient to sign*, which is generally the case, the time in which the cancer would have proved fatal may be reduced to a few days. There is also a difference in tumors: some under no circumstances cause death; others are liable to become as fatal as a malignant pustule.

In supposed injuries to the joints, the exact cause of the swelling is not always easily determined; and internal abscesses have sometimes been months in reaching a condition which would enable the most skilful physicians and surgeons to locate them, or decide positively their cause. The converse of this is true, that swellings have been supposed to be caused by abscesses, incisions made, and a totally different and comparatively harmless condition found. Hence it is by no means certain that an external disease is properly named. The patient and his attending physicians may be in serious error as to the exact character of what at a first glance it might be supposed easy to identify.

I have already spoken of the power of hysteria to simulate the symptoms of any internal disease. It may be new to some that it can produce very remarkable external developments. On the authority of Dr. Marvin R. Vincent, of this city, I give the following. Says Dr. Vincent: "I was told of a case at St. Luke's Hospital in this city: a woman with a swelling which was pronounced by the physicians to be an ovarian tumor, but which disappeared on the administration of ether, and was discovered to be merely the result of hysteria."

Consumption is a subject of painful interest to almost every family in the country. The peculiarity of this disease is that it advances and retreats. In the more common form there comes a time when what is commonly called softening of the tubercles takes place. The patient is then very ill; hectic fever with the succeeding chill occurs every day, and sometimes several times a day; night-sweats, profuse expectoration, and other evidences and causes of debility complicate the situation, and the end is thought to be not far off. To the surprise of the friends, in a few days he greatly improves. Night-sweats cease, the fever greatly diminishes or disappears, the cough lessens; he rejoices, perhaps resumes his business and receives congratulations. Whatever he had been taking now has the credit,—whether what his physician prescribed or hypophosphites, cod-liver oil, balsams, pectorals, expectorants, "compound oxygen," benzoic; when the fact is that the tubercles have softened. As foreign bodies they produced fever and other symptoms; they have been eliminated by coughing and other natural processes. Meanwhile others are forming which give no uneasiness except a slight increase of shortness of breath. When the second softening period comes the patient sinks lower than before; new remedies, of course, are tried, radical change of diet is made, but if death does not end the scene similar apparent recovery takes place. At either of these stages a visit to a grotto, the operations of "faith-healers," or a magnetic belt or pad, might seem to produce a great effect; but decline would occur at the periods of softening, and the patient afterward improve or sink beyond the possibility of recovery, if none of these things had been done.

A fact concerning consumption is known to medical men and stated in works on hygiene, but often disbelieved. That fact is that pulmonary consumption, genuine and unmistakable, often terminates spontaneously in recovery, and frequently yields to hygienic methods. It is the opinion of one of the most celebrated physicians of Europe that for every two cases of death from consumption there is one case that is either indefinitely prolonged, the patient living to be old, or entirely recovering and dying of old age, or of some entirely different disease. It may be asked how such a fact as this can be established. By two modes—one probable, the other conclusive. The probable is where the patient had all the external symptoms of the disease, and examination of the lungs by competent specialists gave results which agreed with each other and with the external symptoms, and the patient, by changing from a sedentary to an outdoor and active life, entirely recovers and lives for many years without return of the symptoms. Possibility of error in the diagnosis remains, but where all these conditions exist it is reduced to a minimum. Such cases are numerous. Conclusive demonstration is found in post-mortem examinations. The late Prof. Austin Flint of New York, author of the "Practice of Medicine," was also the author of a "Clinical Report on Consumption," and describes sixty-two cases in which an arrest of the disease took place; in seven cases it occurred without any special medical or hygienic treatment, and in four of the seven he declares that recovery was complete.

Prof. J. Hughes Bennett, of the Royal Infirmary at Edinburgh, in a lecture says: "Up to a recent period the general opinion has been that consumption almost always marches on to a fatal termination, and that the cases of those known to be restored were so few as to be merely an exception to the general rule. Morbid anatomy has now, I think, demonstrated that tubercles in an early stage degenerate and become abortive with extreme frequency, in the proportion of one third to one half of all the incurables who die over forty."

Both the Edinburgh "Journal of Medical Science" and the London "Lancet" indorse this conclusion. It is equivalent to saying that from one third to one half of all the incurables of Scotland who die over forty have had incipient consumption and got well of it. To meet those who would say that practically consumption does not mean the existence of a few isolated tubercles, but an advanced stage in which the lungs are in a state of ulceration, and the powers are so lowered that perfect recovery seldom or never takes place, Dr. Bennett proceeds to say that "Laennec, Andral, Cruveilhier, Kingston, Pressat, Boudet, and many others have published cases where all the functional symptoms of the disease, even in its most advanced state, were present, and yet the individual lived many years and ultimately died of some other disorder, and on dissection cicatrices and concretions have been found in the lungs." In that lecture Prof. Bennett exhibited the lungs of a man who died suddenly of congestion of the brain, aged fifty years. At twenty-two he had been given up to die of pulmonary consumption, recovered, lived nearly thirty years, and his lungs exhibited most indubitable marks of the progress and termination of the disease. It is easy to see that in such cases of recovery there came a time when the last tubercles softened; at such a time, any powerful mental stimulus, or pleasing change in circumstances, or physical stimulant compelling exercise in the open air, might be the element which would decide the question whether the system would rally or the process of innutrition and decay go on.

The heating of the minds of witnesses by a succession of testimonies must not be forgotten.

In one of the meetings conducted by the Rev. A. B. Simpson, I heard witnesses testify to the healing power of God, and one witness, who seemed to be a pillar and was specially called upon by Mr. Simpson, testified, stating that no one had greater reason to praise God than he, "for during the past year I have *several* times been *miraculously* and *instantaneously* raised from the *jaws of death.*"

In Adelaide, Australia, at a meeting held in the Workmen's Hall, which was crowded, a Mrs. Morgan testified that for twenty years she had suffered from heart-disease, but the moment "Mr. Wood laid his curative hands upon me, I felt a quiet within and was conscious I was cured." The Rev. W. B. Shorthouse tendered some wonderful testimony; he described his own career of weakness which interfered with his ministerial duties, but now he was completely restored to health. Only two weeks previous, he said, some of his congregation told him that he looked like death. As he grew warm in his testimony, he described several marvelous cases, *one of a man brought in dead* who walked away without assistance. He had seen hundreds "touch the border of Mr. Wood's garment," and finally concluded by saying he was himself "a *living example of miracles greater than those performed by the disciples of Christ.*"

After seeing this in "Galignani's Messenger" in Paris, I ascertained from high authority in Australia that these narratives were greatly exaggerated, and that many relapses had occurred.

If such dangers exist in connection with the testimony of witnesses in religious meetings to *physical facts*, it may be thought that accounts of cases carefully written by honest men might be taken without so many grains of allowance. Having inquired into several of the most conspicuous with whose subjects I am acquainted, I have found that the condition of the patient *prior to the alleged cure* has been magnified in the description. This has not always been so, but in most of the celebrated cases which I have personally investigated.

Many important facts have been omitted, sometimes because the witness did not regard them as of consequence; in other cases, it must be confessed, because the luster of the cure would be dimmed by their recital. A female evangelist, whose astonishing cure has been told to thousands, never mentions a surgical operation from which her friends know that she derived great benefit; and when asked why she did not tell of that, she replied, in substance, that she did not wish to divert attention from the great work that God had really wrought in her. Often the account of the *cure* has been exaggerated: relapses have not been published, peculiar sensations still felt, and resisted, have been omitted from the description, and the mode of the cure has been restricted to one act or a single moment of time, when in response to questions it appeared that it was weeks or months before the person could properly be said to be well. In all such cases it is obvious that the written testimony is of little value; indeed, it is seldom that a published account in books supporting marvels of this kind shows any signs of being written by a person who took the pains, if he possessed the capacity, to investigate the facts accurately. Frequent quotation of such accounts adds nothing to their credibility or value.

But after all deductions have been made, that most extraordinary recoveries have been produced, some of them instantaneously, from disease in some cases generally considered to be incurable by ordinary treatment, in others known to be curable in the ordinary process of medicine and in surgery only by slow degrees, must be admitted.

The object of these remarks is not to discredit all testimony, but to show the conditions upon which its value depends.

EXPLANATION OF THE FACTS

HAVE these facts a common cause? To solve the problem requires us to ascertain whether the effects are the same, and the limitations of the cause or causes are the same? Do recoveries under the prayers and anointings of Dr. Cullis surpass in the nature of disease, rapidity of cure, and proportion of recoveries to the whole number of persons prayed for, those attested in connection with Mrs. Mix or those of the Rev. A. B. Simpson? Is there any reason to believe that Dr. Newton was less successful in the number, character, or permanence of the cures attributed to his touch and voice than those of the persons before named? Again, is there any testimony that they have achieved greater success than "Bethshan" in London? Further, can these be proved to have done any more than Prince Hohenlohe, or the priest Gassner, or the water of Lourdes? The subjects of these cures will, of course, chant the praises of the respective schools; but does the impartial student of the testimony see any reason to distinguish between them as to the number or character of the effects? They all sometimes cure paralysis, convulsions, cancers, tumors, spinal diseases, those peculiar to women, and relieve or cure chronic cases frequently, especially rheumatism, sciatica, neuralgia, and similar maladies. They succeed in some forms of acute disease. "Schools" in religion and medicine are prone to magnify their own achievements and depreciate those of others. Nor does this always spring from dishonesty; since faith often prevents that scrutiny which would reveal reasons for discounting testimony or appearances, while suspicion would lead to a treatment of the reports of others the opposite of that accorded to their own. I have seen subjects of spiritualist healers, mesmeric and magnetic healers, Roman Catholic and Russo-Greek miracles, and of the most conspicuous "faith-healers" and "mind-curers" in this country, and find no reason to believe that one has been more or less successful than others.

A very important question is whether their *limita-*

tions are the same. The limitations must have respect to what and how they heal, and the permanence of the cure. It will be noted that none of them can raise the dead, or if any profess ability to do so, or by prayer to restore to life, the rest will unite to deny the claim of the others, and so fully support our view. Nor can they give sight to one born blind, nor healing to one born deaf, where the cause of deafness is the absence of any of the organs necessary to hearing. Instances have been published where children who had lost their hearing by scarlet fever or other disease, have been made to hear by the manipulations of spiritualists or by the prayers of Catholics or Protestants; but whether true or not, no case which can be shown to be one of congenital deafness or blindness can be attested where sight or hearing has been made possible by any other than surgical treatment. Further, none of them can restore a limb that has been cut off, or an eye that has been lost.

In mental derangement it is to be admitted that all have been successful in some cases of a functional character, and in some of protracted melancholia; but no authentic account has been adduced of the cure of dementia or idiocy.

Another common limitation is the existence of many cases of the same disease in which cures are effected, which they cannot relieve in the least. Pitiful instances could be detailed of persons who have traveled long distances, or have believed in the water, or the power of the dead body of an ecclesiastic, or of prayers at his tomb, or of the mystic touch of Newton, or of Dr. Cullis, or of a coterie who have made their headquarters at a famous resort on the coast of the Atlantic, and have died bitterly disappointed. Many have died while firmly believing that God would heal them, and that they were not about to die. Neither

Catholic, Spiritualist, nor Protestant has any preeminence with regard to this limitation.

A remarkable attempt to Christianize the interior of Africa is now proceeding under the auspices of William Taylor, a missionary bishop. One of the company which he took out was an obstinate believer in the power of faith to draw from God such help as to enable him to dispense with medicine. This young man fanatically refused to take any medicine, and died a martyr to superstition which he mistook for faith. The last entry in his diary was: "I have n't the fever, but a weak feeling; but I take the promise 'He giveth power to the faint,' and I do receive the fact." The testimony of his medical adviser to his last conversation is: "Charlie, your temperature is 105, and pulse 130; normal is 98; the dividing line between life and death is 103. You are now dying. It is only a question of time; and if you do not take something to break up this fever, it will surely kill you." The reply of the misguided youth was, "Well, then, I'll die; for I won't take any medicine." Bishop Taylor himself does not hold the view which, consistently carried out, practically caused the suicide of this young man. Almost all in the party had the African fever, and by the aid of medical skill recovered.

The limitations common to all are further illustrated by the following case, an account of which I received in writing from the eminent physician who had it in charge until the fatal termination. A minister of the gospel and his wife, widely known both in Europe and America, had a daughter-in-law to whom they were greatly attached. Her health began to fail, and all that medical treatment could do was done without avail. The diagnosis was one of ovarian tumor, and little hope was offered either to the invalid or to her friends. Finally she was made a subject of prayer by the minister and his wife, who earnestly besought God to heal her. They believed that they received an evidence in answer to their prayers that she would be cured; but being about to make a long evangelizing tour throughout the world, they prayed that if she was to get well, they might receive a certain sign which they suggested in prayer; and the event was in harmony with the suggestion. Thoroughly persuaded, they made a farewell visit and had a season of prayer in which both they and she received "the assurance" that the disease was checked, and that she would finally recover. Previous to their embarking on the voyage, at a meeting which was attended by thousands, her case was spoken of and prayers were offered for her recovery; and this happened on several occasions during the long tour following. But the disease progressed and ended in death, according to the prognosis given by the physician, who is himself a Christian. These facts show the deceptive character of the assurances which many claim to receive on matters of fact of this kind.

Another element of limitation has respect to relapses. In many cases those who suppose that they have been cured relapse and die of the malady of which they testified they had been cured. This is true of the results of medical practice, and is a consequence of the law of human mortality and general limitations of human knowledge; but it is specially true of quack medicines involving anodynes, alcohol, or other stimulants which disguise symptoms, develop latent energy, or divert attention.

Lord Gardenstone, himself a valetudinarian, spent a great deal of time "inquiring for those persons who had actually attested marvelous cures, and found that more than two thirds of the number died very shortly after they had been cured." That the proportion of relapses among persons who have attested cures under the Spiritualists, Magnetizers, Roman Catholics, and Protestants is as great as this, I do not affirm; but I have no doubt that it is greater than among those who have supposed themselves to be cured either by hygienic means without medicine, or under the best attainable medical treatment, which always attends to hygiene in proportion to the intellectual and moral elevation of the physician above the sphere of quackery.

Some years since a member of the Christian church in the city of Boston solemnly testified that he had been entirely cured of pulmonary consumption through the anointing and prayer of Dr. Cullis. In less than six months afterward he died of consumption. "Zion's Herald," a paper published in the same city, in an editorial upon the results of a faith-healing convention at Old Orchard, says: "We are not surprised to learn that some who esteemed themselves healed are suffering again from their old infirmities, in some instances more severely than before." Such relapses are exceedingly numerous, but they are not published; the jubilant testimonies are telegraphed throughout the land and dilated upon in books; the subsequent relapses are not spoken of in religious meetings nor published anywhere, but a little pains enabled me in a single year to collect a large number.

If we are not able to conclude a common cause from these concurrences in effects, limitations, and relapses, neither the deductive nor the inductive process is of value, and all modes of acquiring knowledge or tracing causes would seem to be useless.

But what is that common cause? Can these effects be proved to be natural by constructing a formula by which they can be produced? If there be phenomena in which the results cannot be traced to their sources, can they be shown to be similar to other effects whose causes can be thus traced?

In investigating phenomena, some of which it is claimed are connected with religion and others with occult forces, it is necessary to proceed *without regard to the question of religion*, in determining whether the facts can be accounted for upon natural principles, and paralleled by the application thereof.

In searching for analogies I avail myself of authentic cases found in John Hunter, in Dr. Tuke's work previously referred to, in the "Mental Physiology" of Dr. Carpenter, and in the psychological researches of Sir Benjamin Brodie and Sir Henry Holland; selecting, however, only such facts as have been paralleled under my own observation.

First. Cases where the effect is unquestionably produced by a natural mental cause.

(a) The charming away of warts is well established. Dr. Tuke says of them: "They are so apparent that there cannot be much room for mistake as to whether they have or have not disappeared, and in some instances within my own knowledge their disappearance was in such close connection with the psychical treatment adopted, that I could hardly suppose the cure was only *post hoc*. In one case, a relative of mine had a troublesome wart on the hand, for which I made use of the usual local remedies, but without effect. After they were discontinued, it remained *in statu quo* for some time, when a gentleman 'charmed' it away in a few days." He then tells of a case the particulars of which he received of a surgeon. His daughter had about a dozen warts on her hands, and they had been there eighteen months; her father had applied caustic and other remedies without success. A gentlemen called, noticed her warts, and asked how many she had. She said she did not know, but thought about a dozen. "Count them, will you?" said he, and solemnly took down her counting, remarking, "You will not be troubled with your warts after next Sunday." Dr. Tuke adds, "It is a fact that by the day named the warts had disappeared and did not return." Francis Bacon had a similar experience, including the removal of a wart which had been with him from childhood, on which he says: "At the rest I did little marvel, because they came in a short time, and might go away in a short time again; but the going away of that which had stayed so long doth yet stick with me."

(b) Blood-diseases, such as scurvy, have been cured in the same way. At the siege of Breda in 1625, scurvy prevailed to such an extent that the Prince of Orange was about to capitulate. The following experiment was resorted to: "Three small phials of medicine were given to each physician, not enough for recovery of two patients. It was publicly given out that three or four drops were sufficient to impart a healing virtue to a gallon of liquor." Dr. Frederic Van der Mye, who was present and one of the physicians, says: "The effect of the delusion was really astonishing; for many quickly and perfectly recovered. Such as had not moved their limbs for a month before were seen walking the streets, sound, upright, and in perfect health." Dr. Van der Mye says that before this happy experiment was tried they were in a condition of absolute despair, and the scurvy and the despair had produced "fluxes, dropsies, and every species of distress, attended with a great mortality."

(c) Van Swieten and Smollett speak of consumptive patients recovering health from falling into cold water. Dr. Tuke says that Dr. Rush refers to these cases, and "inclines to think that fright and the consequent exertion produced a beneficial result."

(d) Abernethy gives a case of a woman who was permanently cured of dropsy by being frightened by a bull, relief coming through the kidneys.

(e) Of the famous metallic tractors of Dr. Perkins, which produced most extraordinary results, attracting the attention of the medical world, the effects of the use of the tractors being attributed to galvanism, and of the production of the same effects by two wooden tractors of nearly the same shape, and painted so as to resemble them in color, it is hardly necessary to say anything. But wooden and metallic were equally efficient, and cured cases of chronic rheumatism in the ankle, knee, wrist, and hip, where the joints were swollen and the patient had been ill for a long time; and even a case of lockjaw of three or four days' standing was cured in fifty minutes, when the physicians had lost all hope.

(f) I have frequently tested this principle. The application of a silver dollar wrapped in silk to ulcerated teeth, where the patient had been suffering for many hours, and in some instances for days, relieved the pain, the patient supposing that it was an infallible remedy. After I had explained that the effect was wholly mental, the magic power of the remedy was gone.

(g) In 1867 a well-known public singer was taken dangerously ill on the evening of his concert, having great nausea and intense headache; two applications of the silver dollar to his forehead entirely relieved him, and he performed a full program with his usual energy. Anything else would have been as effectual as the dollar, which was used merely because it was at hand.

(h) The following case is taken from a pamphlet published by me in 1875, entitled "Supposed Miracles."

In company with the Rev. J. B. Faulks I called at a place near Englewood, N. J., to procure a boat. There was a delay of half an hour, and the day being chilly, we repaired to a house near by and there saw a most pitiable spectacle. The mother of the family was suffering from inflammatory rheumatism in its worst form. She was terribly swollen, could not move, nor bear to be touched. I said to Mr. Faulks, "You shall now have an illustration of the truth of the theory you have so often heard me advance." He mildly demurred, and intimated that he did not wish to be mixed up in anything of the kind. But, after making various remarks solely to inspire confidence and expectation, I called for a pair of knitting-needles. After some delay, improved to increase confidence and surround the proceedings with mystery, operations were begun. One of the hands of the patient was so swollen that the fingers were very nearly as large as the wrist of an ordinary child three years of age. In fact, almost all the space naturally between the fingers was occupied, and the fist was clinched. It was plain that to open them voluntarily was impossible, and to move them intensely painful. The daughter informed us that the hand had not been opened for several weeks. When all was ready I held the needle about two inches from the end of the woman's fingers, just above the clinched hand, and said, "Now, Madam, do not think of your fingers, and above all do not try to move them, but fix your eyes on the ends of these needles." She did so, and to her own wonder and that of her daughter the fingers straightened out and became flexible without the least pain. I then moved the needles about, over the hand, and she declared that all pain left her hand except in one spot about half an inch in diameter.

(*i*) The efficacy of the touch of the king to cure scrofula is authenticated beyond question. Charles II. touched nearly 100,000 persons; James in one of his journeys touched 800 persons in Chester Cathedral. Macaulay's History shows how, when William III. refused to exercise this power, it brought upon him "an avalanche of the tears and cries of parents of the children who were suffering from scrofula. Bigots lifted up their hands and eyes in horror at his impiety." His opponents insinuated that he dared not try a power which belonged only to legitimate sovereigns; but this sarcasm was without basis, as an old author says: "The curing of the king's evil by the touch of the king does much puzzle our philosophers, *for whether our kings were of the house of York or Lancaster*, it did cure for the most part." This reminds the student of ecclesiastical history of the consternation of the Jesuits when the extraordinary "miracle" was wrought upon the niece of the famous Blaise Pascal.

(*j*) The daughter of an eminent clergyman in this city had been sick for a long time, entirely unable to move and suffering intense pain. One of the most famous surgeons of New York declared, after careful examination, that she had diseases of the breast-bone and ribs which would require incisions of so severe a character as to be horrible to contemplate. Three times the surgeon came with his instruments to perform the operation, but the parents could not bring themselves to consent to it, and it was postponed. At last the late Dr. Krackowitzer was called in; he solemnly and very thoroughly examined her from head to foot, taking a long time, and at last suddenly exclaimed, "Get out of bed, put on your clothes, and go down-stairs to meet your mother in the parlor!" The young lady automatically arose and obeyed him. The next day she took a walk with her mother, and soon entirely recovered. Dr. Krackowitzer stated that he recognized in her an obstinate case of hysteria, which needed the stimulus of sudden command from a stronger will than her own. I received this narrative from the young lady's father; she has never had a relapse, and is still living in excellent health. Had she been cured by a faith-healer believed in by the family, the mistaken diagnosis of the eminent surgeon would have been heralded far and wide, and the cure considered a miracle.

(k) The cure of obstinate constipation when all medicine had lost its effect, by a medical man who required the patient to uncover the abdomen and direct his thoughts entirely to the sensations experienced in that region, is vouched for by Dr. Carpenter.

(l) The cure of a case of paralysis by Sir Humphrey Davy is a scientific fact of the first importance. He placed a thermometer under the tongue of the patient simply to ascertain the temperature; the patient at once claimed to experience relief, so the same treatment was continued for two weeks, and by that time the patient was well. In this case the imagination of the patient was not assisted by an application to the affected part.

In all the foregoing cases the cure or relief was a natural result of mental or emotional states. As long ago as the time of John Hunter, it was established by a variety of experiments and by his own experience that the concentration of attention upon any part of the human system affects first the sensations, next produces a change in the circulation, then a modification of the nutrition, and finally an alteration in structure.

Second. Cases in which the operation of occult causes is claimed. These will be treated here *only so far as they reflect light upon "faith-cures."*

(*a*) That trances and healings occurred under the performances of Mesmer is as well established as any fact depending upon testimony. French scientists who investigated the subject divided into two hostile parties upon the explanation, and in some cases as to whether they were genuine or fraudulent; but they agreed as to the genuineness of many of the cures. The Government established a commission of physicians and members of the Academy of Sciences to investigate the phenomena. Benjamin Franklin, who was at that time in Paris in the interest of the United States, and the distinguished J. S. Bailly were of that commission, with Lavoisier, Darcet, and others. They presented an elaborate report, specifically admitting many of the alleged facts, but denying the necessity of assuming "animal magnetism." Forty years afterward,—namely, on October 11, 1825,—the Royal Academy of Medicine in Paris was addressed by a noted physician, Foissac, who called its attention to the importance of a new inquiry. After a long debate the Academy appointed a committee to inquire whether it would or would not become the Academy to investigate "animal magnetism." The report was favorable, and was debated at great length; it was finally decided to investigate, and the Academy, by a majority of ten in a total vote of sixty, appointed a permanent committee on the subject. This committee reaffirmed the facts, and did not divide as in the former instance, two merely declining to sign the report because not present at the experiments. The subject was reopened in 1837, and further reports and discussions of great importance resulted. These are referred to here simply to show the amount of testimony to certain facts of trance conditions, so called, and cures.

The following is given on the authority of Dr. Tuke, who says, "It is afforded by a highly respectable surgeon and attributed by him to mesmerism." It is the case of Edward Wine, aged seventy-five, who had been paralyzed two years in one arm and leg. The left arm was spasmodically fixed to the chest, the fingers drawn toward the palm of the hand and wasted, quite incapable of holding anything; walked with a crutch, drawing the left leg after him. After several mesmerizing operations the surgeon put "a nosegay in his coat and posted him off to church, and he tells me he walked like a gentleman down the aisle, carrying his stick in his lame arm."

The noted Mr. Braid in many authentic instances restored lost sight, greatly improved the condition of the paralyzed, in some instances entirely curing the patient, and had very little difficulty with most cases of rheumatism. Dr. W. B. Carpenter investigated many of these cases.

But what is mesmerism, magnetism, electro-biology, etc.? It is a subjective condition. The notion that a magnetic fluid passes from the body, or that passes are of utility in producing the state except as they act upon the mind of the candidate, was exploded long since; and both in Europe and America the discovery of the real principle was accidental and made by a number of persons. About fifty years ago an itinerant lecturer on these phenomena, who had great success in experiments, used an old-fashioned cylinder electrical machine. The "subjects" took hold of the wire. He gave them a slight electrical shock, and "concentrated his will upon them." Those that were susceptible passed into the trance state. On a certain occasion, when trying the experiment with several gentlemen in a private room, the operator was called out just as the candidates had taken hold of the wire. He remained twenty minutes, not supposing that the experiment was being tried; on his return, to his great surprise, he found three of them as much "magnetized," "mesmerized," electro-biologized," "hypnotized," or "psycodunamized" as any he had ever seen. This showed that the entire effect was caused by their own mental states. Further experiments made it clear that neither the will of the operator, nor any "magnetism" from his body, nor electricity, nor the influence of the candidates upon each other had anything to do with the result. Mesmer himself used magnets until he fell in with the Roman Catholic priest Gassner, before mentioned, when, perceiving that he used none, he renounced magnets, afterward depending solely on manipulation.

Twenty-three years ago I was present at a private meeting of twenty-five ladies and gentlemen, at the residence of Mr. Henry R. Towne, president of the Yale and Towne Manufacturing Company. On two successive evenings these phenomena had been explained. It had been maintained that all the results were subjective, arising from the concentrated attention, expectancy, and reverence of the persons trying the experiment. At the close of the two lectures, after divesting the subject of mystery, and, apparently, rendering it impossible to produce reverence or confidence, I was urged to test the theory by experiment. Accordingly eight gentlemen and ladies were requested to rise, stand without personal contact with one another or myself, close their eyes, and clasp their hands. In a few minutes five passed more or less fully into the trance state, two becoming unconscious of their surroundings and the others exhibiting peculiar phenomena. One thus affected was a

prominent lawyer of the city of New York, another
a recent graduate of the Sheffield Scientific School,
and the third the bookkeeper in a large establishment. *Nothing* was done by the experimenter during
the interval after these persons closed their eyes and
clasped their hands, save to wait in silence and require silence from spectators. Among those who witnessed and critically studied these phenomena with
the writer were Professor Fuertes, Dean of the Department of Civil Engineering in Cornell University,
whose letter, herewith printed,[1] explains itself; Mr.
Henry R. Towne, before mentioned; the Rev. Dr.

[1] DR. J. M. BUCKLEY. DEAR SIR: My recollection of the
"séance" referred to in your letter of the 25th ult. is not as
distinct in some points as in others you do not mention. The
study of psychology is so important that it is necessary to be
exact beyond measure in order not to mislead. An immense
amount of rubbish has been piled upon slender foundations in
the study of psycho-genesis, and no progress can be made so
long as people assent easily to become witnesses with external aid to recollect facts which happened long ago. I am very
positive as to the truth of the following facts: I belonged to a
literary club, composed of the most cultivated people residing
in Stamford in 1864-71. At one of our meetings, I was present
when you performed some experiments upon ten or fifteen of its
members by asking them to stand in a circle, with closed eyes,
and holding their hands before their faces as in the conventional attitude for praying; the gas was partly turned down.
Some of the members of this group laughed, and you peremptorily excluded them from the circle, as previously agreed upon. A
short time afterward one of my neighbors began to breathe hard,
and he was followed by several others, who gave indications,
plainly visible, that something unusual was happening to them.

If human testimony is to be depended upon at all, I am sure
that the social position of the persons so affected, their high
culture, refinement, and surroundings, entitled their actions to
be believed, as representing truthfully the conditions causing
their strange behavior, even if the following circumstances did
not reinforce the necessity of believing their candid sincerity in
this question. One of the first "subjects" was a young lady,

A. S. Twombly, pastor of the Winthrop Congregational Church of Charlestown, Mass.; and J. B. Williams, Esquire, of the city of New York.

On the 14th of April, 1868, in the City Hall of Dover, New Hampshire, in the presence of a thousand persons, the same principles were set forth. At the close Dr. L. G. Hill, of that city, long President of the State Medical Society, called for the proof of the theory that the effects attributed to animal magnetism were the result of subjective mental condition. The result, as described in the "Dover Gazette" of Friday, April 17, 1868, by the editor, who refers to himself in the account, is as follows: "Ten or twelve gentlemen at his [the lecturer's] request took the platform and were requested to shut their eyes, close their hands, and remain quiet. They did so. One complete trance medium and two partial ones at once developed.

who was made to believe that she was writing a letter to a friend, and immediately began to simulate the act of writing; but other subjects proving to be most amusingly affected, she was, unfortunately, forgotten, and allowed to go on "writing" for nearly three hours consecutively, earnestly engaged at her task, oblivious of her surroundings, neither laughing, nor apparently caring for what was going on. The effect of holding her hand in mid-air for so long a time, and moving her fingers all the time, is a feat of endurance of which she was not physically able, if conscious. Her arm and shoulder were swollen and lame for several days after this performance. [Owing to the crowded condition of the room, I did not observe this till the interview terminated. AUTHOR.] Another subject was a young lady who had recently lost a friend. The mother of her dead friend had also recently arrived from Europe and was present in the room; and after the young lady affected had expressed her ability to go to heaven and described what she saw there, she paused a moment, as if surprised and filled with terror; then, uttering a piercing scream, moved forward as if to embrace the dead friend, whose name she mentioned, in a manner so tragic and out of keeping with her usual lovely and bashful demeanor that the impression produced on the company was quite pro-

Three of the other gentlemen, among whom was the writer of this article, felt the trance force in a slight degree. The completely developed medium was in the most perfect trance; could be convinced of anything at once; was clairvoyant, ecstatic, mesmeric, somnambulic, and in fact took any form of ideomania at will. We have been at perhaps over a hundred séances of mesmeric, biologic, and so-called spiritual subjects or mediums, but have never seen so perfect a subject so soon developed and upon so pure a principle." These cases are adduced to show the effect of the mind upon the body, and of the mind upon its own faculties. The young man particularly mentioned by the "Gazette" could have had every tooth extracted, or even a limb amputated, without consciousness. After he had resumed his normal state, such was his susceptibility that a word would have sent him back to sleep.

found. This behavior, both brutal and coarse, and cruel to the mother of the dead young girl, is, I am very sure, incompatible with any theory of Miss —— being in her usual senses. In fact she was made ill by this circumstance, and conceived the greatest aversion toward you. Her friend had been buried but a few days. [These facts were unknown to me, and as soon as possible her attention was diverted from them. As the whole was imaginary, this was easily done. AUTHOR.]

One of the most amusing incidents was the honest conviction with which a prominent lawyer believed himself sitting on a log looking into the muddy bottom of a stream of water. Another, that of a young man whose trembling legs were made to bend under the enormous weight of an envelope placed over his head, when told it weighed a ton. The above are a few of the things I saw about which I am positive my memory of the events is perfect. Also, that you stated that you would not and did not exercise any act of volition or influence upon your "subjects," but merely waited for them to fall into the hypnotic state giving rise to the phenomena described.

Believe me, sincerely,
E. A. Fuertes.

ITHACA, NEW YORK, January 30, 1886.

If he had been ill of any disease which "faith-healers" or "magnetizers" could relieve, he would have received equal help. While these persons were standing and the susceptible were passing "under the influence," I was *simply waiting*, "only this and nothing more."

(*b*) As for causing the bedridden to rise, and breaking up morbid conditions that had defied medicine while being aggravated by it, these are among the simplest applications of the principle involved. The confidence of those unfamiliar with the subject would be taxed beyond endurance by the narration of illustrative facts to which there is abundant testimony and which can be paralleled easily.

(*c*) Intelligent missionaries and travelers in heathen lands, where they have given any investigation to the subject, unite in testifying that extraordinary cures follow the enchantments and magical rites employed by priests and physicians claiming supernatural powers.

(*d*) The influence of witch-doctors among the negroes of Africa, both to produce disease and cure it, is as well authenticated as any facts concerning the "Dark Continent"; nor is it necessary to go there for illustrations, which can be found in great numbers in the South. Not long since an entire community in the vicinity of Atlanta, Georgia, were greatly excited by the terrible diseases which followed threats made by a doctor of this sort. Voodooism has power to bring on diseases and also to cure; nor need this burden be placed upon the negroes and American Indians exclusively. In various parts of Austria, Germany, and Russia, among the peasantry and ignorant classes, belief in witchcraft, and the coincidences which sustain it, still exists; and on the authority of most distinguished physicians and surgeons in those

FAITH-HEALING 33

countries, I state that the results both in inflicting and in removing what they never inflicted, which follow the operations of these witch-doctors, are often astonishing.

(e) There is an old proverb that "when rogues fall out, honest men get their dues." It is also true that when quacks fall to discrediting each other, principles may be discovered. In 1865 there came to Detroit, Michigan, a pupil of Dr. Newton, Bryant by name, who performed cures as successfully as Newton himself. In company with Dr. J. P. Scott, a Presbyterian minister there, I visited Dr. Bryant, and saw him operate upon a score or more of patients (one of whom had been supposed to be doomed to a speedy death with ovarian tumor; Dr. Bryant removed the tumor, after which she lived some months and died of debility). To comprehend his methods fully I was operated upon for dyspepsia. About a year later, returning from New Orleans to Memphis, Tennessee, I found on board the steamer Dr. Newton, who had just come from Havana. He told me that in one day eight hundred persons had applied to him in that city. On the same steamer was Dr. B—— of St. Louis, an aged physician who had been to Havana with a wealthy patient. I inquired of Dr. B—— and others whether such great numbers had visited Dr. Newton, and was told that such was the report, that vast crowds had surrounded him from the day he arrived till he embarked, and that marvelous tales were told of the cures he performed. For several hours a day during four days I conversed with him concerning his career and principles. My conviction is that he believed in himself, and also that he would use any means to accomplish his ends. He would glide from fanaticism into hypocrisy, then into fanaticism, and from that into common sense, with the rapidity of thought. He said that he was influenced by spirits who told him what to say. He would use the name of Jesus Christ in what would seem a blasphemous manner; standing before an audience he would say, "I am now about to send forth shocks of vitality." He would move his arms backward and forward and exclaim, "In the name of Jesus Christ, I command the diseases in the persons now present to disappear!" He would go to the paralytic or lame and exclaim, "In the name of Jesus Christ, be healed of your infirmity." When I mentioned having seen "Dr." Bryant, Dr. Newton instantly denounced him as an "unmitigated fraud who had no genuine healing power." He claimed that he had cured Bryant of a malignant disease with which he found him suffering in a hospital; that Bryant had acted as his amanuensis for some time, and then left him, and had since been acting in opposition to him. Knowing that the manipulations by Bryant had been followed by some wonderful results in Detroit, I said to Dr. Newton:

"If Bryant be an unmitigated fraud, how do you account for his cures?"

"Oh!" said the doctor, "they are caused by the faith of the people and the concentration of their minds upon his operations, with the expectation of being cured. Now," said he, "none would go to see Bryant unless they had some faith that he might cure them, and when he begins his operations with great positiveness of manner, and they see the crutches he has, and hear the people testify that they have been cured, it produces a tremendous influence upon them; and then he gets them started in the way of exercising, and they do a good many things they thought they could not do; their appetites and spirits revive, and if toning them up can possibly reduce the diseased tendency, many of them will get well."

Said I, "Doctor, pardon me, is not that a correct account of the manner in which you perform your wonderful works?"

"Oh, no," said he; "the difference between a genuine healer and a quack like Bryant is as wide as the poles."

To question him further upon this line would have put an end to the conversation sooner than I desired.

But testing fundamentally the same methods before and since that interview on many occasions, always under the great disadvantage of not being able to profess supernatural aid, either of spirits or of God, and thus being shut up to affecting the mind by the laws of suggestion and association, and by the manner assumed, and finding a result similar in kind, and in some cases equal in extent, to any produced by Newton or others, I know that when he was explaining to me the success of Bryant upon the assumption that he had no healing power, he gave inadvertently the whole explanation of the healing as far as it is independent of mere physical manipulation. Dr. Newton had been to Havana with his daughter, very low with consumption. He was taking her North, doubtful if she would reach home alive. On my saying, "Doctor, why could you not heal her?" he mournfully replied, "It seems as if we cannot always affect our own kindred!"

(*f*) In working miraculous cures, the Mormons are fully equal to Catholics or Protestants. In Europe one of their chief methods of making converts is praying with the sick, who often recover; and similar success has often aided them in making converts in this country. The Rev. Nathaniel Mead, a highly respected clergyman, to whom Dr. Baird refers in his "History of the Town of Rye," authorized me to publish the following facts, with the sanction of his name.

In the year 1839 a Mormon priest came to the neighborhood where Mr. Mead resided, and obtained access to the room of an intelligent member of a Christian church, who had long been hopelessly ill. He asked permission to pray for her. Catching at anything, she consented. He prayed with great earnestness, and she at once began to improve and recovered with surprising rapidity. Convinced by the supposed miracle that God was with the Mormon priest, she left the Christian church and identified herself with the Mormons to the extent of deserting friends and home.

In the same locality, another member of a Christian church had been severely injured by a bar of iron which fell upon his foot, mangling and crushing it. The same Mormon priest prayed with him, with a similar result; the wound healed very soon, and the man became a convert to Mormonism.

So great was the faith of certain Mormon proselytes in Europe that the priesthood could work miracles, that one who had lost a leg and could not secure another through the prayers of the Mormon missionaries, crossed the Atlantic and made a pilgrimage to Salt Lake City, where he had an interview with Brigham Young. This fox-like prophet and miracle-worker, who could cope in intellectual keenness with Horace Greeley, said to him, "It would be easy for me to give you another leg, but it is my duty to explain to you the consequences. You are now well advanced in life. If I give you another leg, you will indeed have two legs until you die, which will be a great convenience; but in the resurrection, not only will the leg which you lost rise and be united to your body, but also the one which I now give you; thus you will be encumbered with three legs throughout eternity. It is for you to decide whether you would prefer the transient inconvenience of getting along with one leg till you die, or, the deformity of an extra leg forever." The pilgrim concluded to remain maimed in this life, that he might not be deformed in that which is to come. This may be a myth, but it falls in well with Brigham Young's known character, and is as worthy of respect as the reasons given by professedly Christian faith-healers for not working miracles of this kind, which are that they do not find "any special promise for such cases," and that "they find no instance where the apostles gave new limbs."

INDUCTIONS

THE inductions from these cases, and from the fact that they are constantly paralleled, are:

(1) That subjective mental states, such as concentration of the attention upon a part with or without belief, can produce effects either of the nature of disease or cure.

(2) Active incredulity in persons not acquainted with these laws, but willing to be experimented upon, is often more favorable to sudden effects than mere stupid, acquiescent credulity. The first thing the incredulous, hard-headed man, who believes that "there is nothing in it," sees, that he cannot fathom, may lead him to succumb instantly to the dominant idea.

(3) That concentrated attention, with faith, can produce powerful effects; may operate efficiently in acute diseases, with instantaneous rapidity upon nervous diseases, or upon any condition capable of being

modified by direct action through the nervous or circulatory system.

(4) That cures can be wrought in diseases of accumulation, such as dropsy and tumors, with surprising rapidity, where the increased action of the various excretory functions can eliminate morbid growths.

(5) That rheumatism, sciatica, gout, neuralgia, contraction of the joints, and certain inflammatory conditions, may suddenly disappear under similar mental states, so as to admit of helpful exercise; which exercise by its effect upon the circulation, and through it upon the nutrition of diseased parts, may produce a permanent cure.

(6) That the "mind-cure," apart from the absurd philosophy of the different sects into which it is already divided, and its repudiation of all medicine, has a basis in the laws of nature. The pretense of mystery, however, is either honest ignorance or consummate quackery.

(7) That all are unable to dispense with surgery, where the case is in the slightest degree complex and mechanical adjustments are necessary; also that they cannot restore a limb, or eye, or finger, or even a tooth. But in certain displacements of internal organs the consequence of nervous debility, which are sometimes aided by surgery, they all sometimes succeed by developing latent energy through mental stimulus.

THE MIRACLES OF CHRIST AND HIS APOSTLES

WE find that in comparison with the Mormons, Spiritualists, Mind-Curers, Roman Catholics, and Magnetizers, the Protestant Faith-Healers can accomplish as much, but no more; that they have the same limitations as to diseases they cannot heal, and injuries they cannot repair; as to particular cases of diseases that they can generally cure, but which occasionally defy them; and as to their liability to relapses. We also find that their phenomena can be paralleled under the operation of laws with which "experts" upon the subject, whether medical or otherwise, are acquainted, but which are not recognized by the general public, including many physicians of various schools, clergymen, lawyers, educators, and literary persons of both sexes who might be expected to understand them.

It is necessary to examine the New Testament, to ascertain whether Christ was subject to the limitations which have marked all these. The record states that *he* healed "*all* manner of disease, and all manner of sickness." It declares that "they brought unto him *all* that were sick, holden of divers diseases and torments, possessed with devils, and those that were lunatic [new version, epileptic] and palsied; and he healed them." He did these things uniformly, and sent word to John, "The *blind* receive their sight and the *lame* walk, the *lepers* are cleansed and the *deaf* hear, and the *dead are raised up.*" He restored the withered hand, not by the slow process of a change in the circulation, and gradual change in the nutrition, followed by structural alteration; but it was instantly made "whole like as the other." Not only so, he restored limbs that had been cut off. See New Revision, Matthew xv. 30: "And there came unto him great multitudes having with them the lame, blind, dumb, *maimed*, and many others, and they cast them down at his feet; and he healed them; insomuch that the multitude wondered, when they saw the dumb speaking, the *maimed whole*, and the lame walking, and the blind seeing." The last miracle that Christ wrought before his crucifixion, according to St. Luke, was one that could defy all these "faith-healers" of every species to parallel. See New Revision, Luke xxii. 50: "And a certain one of them smote the servant of the high priest and *struck off his right ear*. But Jesus answered and said, Suffer ye thus far. And he touched his ear and *healed him*."

Rational men familiar with the laws expounded in this paper could not believe this record if the mighty works told of Christ and the apostles were comprised simply in an account of wonderful tales. They would reason that it is much more probable that those who testified to these things were deceived or exaggerated, or that those who received the original accounts added to them, than that they should have happened. But when those who make the record convey to us ancient prophecies attested and still preserved by the Jews and fulfilled in the character and works of Christ; the account of his rejection and crucifixion by the Jews; the Sermon on the Mount; the parable of the prodigal son; the Golden Rule; the sublime and spiritual doctrines taught by Christ; and the picture of a life and of a death scene that have no parallel in human history or fiction, and declare that he who taught these things did such and such mighty works before us, we saw them and were convinced by the miracles that he did, "that he was a teacher come from God," it is no longer a question simply of believing things not included in the laws of nature. When these doctrines are applied to men's own needs and lives, they prove their divine origin by the radical and permanent changes which they make in character. Then the subjects of these changes accept the truthfulness of the record of miracles in a remote past which they cannot now test upon the authority of the spiritual truths which they are capable of subjecting to the test of practical experience.

Some allege that even the apostles could not restore limbs that had been cut off, or that had been wanting from birth. The record shows that the apostles made no distinction in cases. Ananias prayed for Paul, and "straightway there fell from his eyes as it had been scales." When Tabitha lay dead, Peter, after prayer, "turning to the body said, 'Tabitha, arise,'" and he "presented her alive." The chains fell off Peter in the prison, and "the iron gate opened for him and the angel of its own accord." As Peter had, in the first miracle after Pentecost, given strength to a man who had been *lame from his mother's womb,* so Paul, seeing a man at Lystra, "a cripple from his mother's womb who had never walked," said, "with a loud voice, 'Stand upright on thy feet,' and he leaped up and walked." They cast out devils wherever it was necessary, and when Eutychus fell from the third story, and "was taken up dead," Paul restored him to life again. On the island of Melita, a viper hung upon the hand of Paul, and "when the barbarians saw the beast hanging from his hand, they said one to another, No doubt this man is a murderer, whom, though he hath escaped from the sea, yet justice hath not suffered to live"; but when they remained long in expectation and beheld nothing amiss come to him, they changed their minds and said he was a "god." We are informed that after that the diseases of the entire population of the island were healed.

CLAIMS OF "CHRISTIAN FAITH-HEALERS," TECHNICALLY SO CALLED, EFFECTUALLY DISCREDITED

In examining the healing works both of Christ and the apostles, it appears that there is not a uniform law that the sick should exercise faith, and that it was not necessary that their friends should exercise it, nor that either they or their friends should do so. Sometimes the sick alone believed; at others, their friends believed and they knew nothing about it; again, both the sick and their friends believed, and on some occasions neither the sick nor the friends. No account of failure on the part of Christ, or of the apostles after his ascension, to cure *any* case can be found. Neither is there a syllable concerning any *relapse* or the danger of such a thing, nor any cautions to the cured, "*not to mind sensations,*" or that "*sensations are tests of faith,*" nor any other such quackery, in the New Testament.

Claims of Christian faith-healers to supernatural powers are discredited by three facts:

(1) They exhibit no supremacy over pagans, spiritualists, magnetizers, mind-curers, etc.

(2) They cannot parallel the mighty works that Christ produced, nor the works of the apostles.

(3) All that they really accomplish can be paralleled without assuming any supernatural cause, and a formula can be constructed out of the elements of the human mind which will give as high average results as their prayers or anointings.

That formula in its lowest form is "*concentrated attention.*" If to this be added reverence, whether for the true and ever-living God, false gods, spirits, the operator, witches, magnetism, electricity, or simple unnamed *mystery*, the effect is increased greatly. If to that be added confident expectancy of particular results, the effect in causing sickness or relieving it may be appalling. Passes, magnets, anointings with oil, are useful only as they produce concentration of attention, reverence, and confident expectancy. Those whose reputation or personal force of thought, manner, or speech can produce these mental states, may dispense with them all, as Mesmer finally did with the "magnets," and as many faith-healers and the Roman Catholics do with the oil.[1]

THE CHRISTIAN DOCTRINE OF ANSWER TO PRAYER

Is there then no warrant in the New Testament for the ordinary Christian to pray for the sick, and is there no utility in such prayers? "There's a Divinity that shapes our ends, rough hew them how we will." The New Testament affirms that "All things work together for good to them that love God." It teaches that the highest good is the knowledge and love of God, and that the Spirit of God has constant access to the minds of men, and sets forth an all-inclusive doctrine of Providence without whom not even a sparrow falls. It does *not* say that prayer will always secure the recovery of the sick, for it gives the instance of Paul who had a "thorn in the flesh," and who besought the Lord thrice that this thing should depart from him, but received, "My grace is sufficient for thee."

None can demonstrate that God cannot work through second causes, bringing about results which, when they come, appear to be entirely natural, but which would not have come except through special providence, or in answer to prayer. The New Testament declares that he does so interpose "according to his will." It was not his will for Paul, and he did not remove the thorn, but gave spiritual blessings instead. Prayer for the sick is one of the most consoling privileges, and it would be a strange omission

---

[1] The Roman Catholics use oil in the "sacrament of extreme unction," which is administered in view of death.

if we were not entitled to pray for comfort, for spiritual help, for such graces as will render continued chastening unnecessary, and for recovery, when that which is desired is in harmony with the will of God. Belief that when the prayer is in accordance with the mind of God, "the prayer of faith shall save the sick, and the Lord shall raise him up," is supported by many explicit promises. But as all who die must die from disease, old age, accident, or intentional violence, every person must at some time be in a state when prayer cannot prolong his life.

When we or others are suffering from any malady, the Christian doctrine is that we are to use the best means at command, and to pray, "Father, if it be possible, let this cup pass from me; nevertheless, not my will but thine be done." The prayer may be answered by its effect upon the mind of the patient; by directing the physician, the nurse, or the friends to the use of such means as may hasten recovery; or, by a direct effect produced upon the physical system, behind the visible system of causes and effects, but reaching the patient through them; if the patient recovers, it will seem as though he recovered naturally, though it may be in an unusual manner. The Christian in his personal religious experience may believe that his prayer was the element that induced God to interfere with the course of nature and prolong life. Assuming that there is a God, who made and loves men, none can show his faith irrational or unscriptural; but such testimony can be of no value to demonstrate to others a fact in the plane of science. When the Christian comes to die, he must then rest, even while praying for life, upon the promise, "My grace is sufficient for thee."

Faith-healers represent God as interfering constantly, not by cause and effect in the order of nature, but affecting the result directly. That they do not surpass those who are not Christians, but use either false pretenses or natural laws, and that they are inferior in healing power to Christ and the apostles, condemn their pretensions. Nor does it avail them to say, "Christ would not come down from the cross when taunted by unbelievers." They might perhaps with propriety refuse a test for *the test's sake;*— though Elijah forced one. But a radical difference between their work and what it accomplishes, and those who, they say, have no divine help, should be manifest. Some of them affirm that the Mormons, Newton, and others do their mighty works by the aid of devils. If so, since casting out devils was miracle-working power of low grade, it is wonderful that none of these persons have been able to cast out the devils from any of the large number who are working in this way, and thus demonstrate their superiority as the apostles vindicated their claims against Simon the sorcerer and others.

Faith-cure, technically so called, as now held by many Protestants, is a pitiable superstition, dangerous in its final effects.

It may be asked, What harm can result from allowing persons to believe in "faith-healing"? Very great indeed. Its tendency is to produce an effeminate type of character which shrinks from pain and concentrates attention upon self and its sensations. It sets up false grounds for determining whether a person is or is not in the favor of God. It opens the door to every superstition, such as attaching importance to dreams; signs; opening the Bible at random, expecting the Lord so to influence their thoughts and minds that they can gather his will from the first passage they see; "impressions," "assurances," etc. Practically it gives support to other delusions which claim a supernatural element. It seriously diminishes the influence of Christianity by subjecting it to a test which it cannot endure. It diverts attention from the moral and spiritual transformation which Christianity professes to work, a transformation which wherever made manifests its divinity, so that none who behold it need any other proof that it is of God. It destroys the ascendancy of reason, and thus, like similar delusions, it is self-perpetuating; and its natural and, in some minds, irresistible tendency is to mental derangement.

Little hope exists of freeing those already entangled, but it is highly important to prevent others from falling into so plausible and luxurious a snare, and to show that Christianity is not to be held responsible for aberrations of the imagination which belong exclusively to no race, clime, age, party, or creed.

DEFENSE OF FAITH-HEALERS EXAMINED

PRESENTATION to the public, through "The Century Magazine," of the substance of the foregoing excited much discussion, and led the most conspicuous advocates of "faith-healing" therein exposed to make such defense as they could. But confident assertions of supernatural powers, and vehement denials of the sufficiency of natural causes to account for their results, and quotations of misapplied passages of Scripture, have been the only defensive weapons of the faith-healers. They have, however, been compelled to avow that "they keep no record of failures, as they do not depend upon phenomena or cases, but upon the divine Word."

This admission is fatal. If they cannot do the works, either they have not the faith, or they misunderstand the promises they quote. Christ and the apostles depended upon the phenomena to sustain their claims; and when the apostles failed in a single instance Christ called them a faithless and perverse generation. The failure of these religious thaumaturgists to surpass other manipulators in the same line in the nature and extent of their mighty works has compelled them to say that they do not depend upon phenomena, and make no record of unsuccessful attempts and relapses.

The difficulty is that they apply promises to the ordinary Christian life which relate to the power of working miracles. That they misunderstand and misapply them is clear also from the fact that most spiritually minded Christians in the greatest emergencies have been unable to work miracles. The reformers—Calvin, Knox, Luther, etc.—could not. John Wesley, in his letter to the Bishop of Gloucester, enumerates all the miraculous gifts possessed by the apostles, and expressly denies that he lays claim to any of them. Judson, Carey, Martyn, Duff, Brainerd,[1] and other eminent missionaries trying to preach the Gospel among Pagans, Mohammedans, and Pantheists, most of whose priests are believed by the people to be able to work miracles, were unable to

[1] Brainerd, in his narrative of his work among the American Indians, confesses his great embarrassment as follows:

"When I have instructed them respecting the miracles wrought by Christ in healing the sick, etc., and mentioned them as evidences of his divine mission, and of the truth of his doctrines, they have quickly referred to the wonders of that kind which [a diviner] had performed by his magic charms, whence they had a high opinion of him and of his superstitious notions, which seemed to be a fatal obstruction to some of them in the way of their receiving the Gospel."

Yet, though Brainerd could do none of these mighty works, he was the means of the conversion of that very diviner by the influence of his own life and the spiritual truths which he taught.

prove their commission by any special power over disease, or by other mighty works. In Algiers, after its conquest by the French, the power of juggling priests was so great that it was impossible to preserve order until Robert Houdin, the magician, was sent over, whose power so far surpassed that of the priests that their ascendancy over the people was broken.

The charge that the writer is not a spiritually minded man was to be expected: this is the common cry of the superstitious when their errors are exposed. But the most extraordinary allegation was made by A. B. Simpson, founder of a sect of faith-healers in the city of New York. He states his belief that the cases "of healing and other supernatural phenomena ascribed to Spiritualism cannot be explained away either as tricks of clever performers or the mere effects of will power, but are, in very many instances, directly supernatural and superhuman"; and asserts that: " The cures to which Dr. Buckley refers among heathen nations, the Voodoos of the negroes, and the Indian medicine men, are all of the same character as Spiritualism." On the subject of Roman Catholic miracles he says:

"Where there is a simple and genuine faith in a Romanist,— and we have found it in some,— God will honor it as well as in a Protestant. . . . But when, on the other hand, they are corrupted by the errors of their Church, and exercising faith, not in God, but in the relics of superstition, or the image of the Virgin, we see no difference between the Romanist and the Spiritualist, and we should not wonder at all if the devil should be permitted to work his lying wonders for them, as he does for the superstitious Pagan or the possessed medium."

This means that if the Roman Catholics are devout, it is God who does the mighty works for them; if superstitious it is the devil. As many of the most remarkable phenomena connected with Roman Catholicism have occurred where the Virgin is most prominent, as at the Grotto of Lourdes, and at Knock Chapel (a girl having been cured recently by drinking water with which some of the mortar of the chapel had been mingled), it is pertinent to ask, if supernatural operations are involved in both, whether the works of God might not be expected to be superior to those of the devil?

Mr. Simpson goes so far as to say that what he calls "divine healing" is "a great practical, Scriptural, and uniform principle, which does not content itself with a few incidental cases for psychological diversion or illustration, but meets the tens of thousands of God's suffering children with a simple practical remedy which all may take and claim if they will." Such propositions as this are as wild as the weather predictions that terrify the ignorant and superstitious, but are the amusement and scorn of all rational and educated persons; as the following, from the "Congregationalist" of Boston, shows:

> We have taken pains, before publishing it, to confirm, by correspondence, the singular case of a woman's death in a religious meeting at Peekskill, N. Y. Rev. Mr. Simpson, formerly a Presbyterian preacher, was holding a Holiness Convention, Major Cole, the "Michigan Evangelist," being a helper. In an "anointing service" an elderly lady, long afflicted with heart-disease, who had walked a long way after a hard day's work, presented herself for "divine healing," and was anointed by Mr. Simpson. A few minutes after she fainted and died, the finding of the jury of inquest being that her death was from heart-disease, but hastened by the excitement of the service. One would suppose that the case would be a warning against the danger of such experiments, if not a rebuke of the almost blasphemous assumption of miraculous power.

ERROR IN MENTAL PHYSIOLOGY

A RADICAL error in mental physiology which most of these persons hold relates to the will. Referring to the theory which explains the cure of many diseases by bringing the person to exercise special will power, Mr. Simpson says:

> Why is it that our physicians and philanthropists cannot get the sick to rise up and exercise this will power? Oh! that is the trouble to which we have already adverted. The will is as weak as the frame, and the power that is needed to energize both is God: and Faith is just another name for the new divine WILL which God breathes into the paralyzed mind, enabling it to call upon the enfeebled body to claim the same divine power for its healing. We are quite willing to admit the blessed effect of a quickened faith and hope and will upon the body of the sick. This is not all. There must also be a direct physical touch.

A hotel-keeper in New Hampshire, lingering at the point of death, as was supposed, for weeks with typhus, saw the flames burst from his barn. "Great God!" cried he, "there is nobody to let the cattle out!" He sprang from the bed, cared for the cattle, broke out in a profuse perspiration, and recovered. The burning barn gave him no strength, but the excitement developed latent energy and will.

Mrs. H. had long been ill, was emaciated and so weak that she could not raise a glass of water to her lips. One day the house took fire. She sprang from the bed, seized a chest full of odds and ends, and carried it out of doors. This, as a result of an effort of will, she could not have done when in health without help.

A letter recently received from the Rev. J. L. Humphrey, for many years a missionary in India, now of Richfield Springs, N. Y., says:

The following instance came under my observation in India. An officer of the Government was compelled to send native messengers out into a district infected with cholera. As he sent them out they took the disease and died; and it came to such a pass among the Government peons under his charge that a man thought himself doomed when selected for that duty. A German doctor in that region had put forth the theory that inoculation with a preparation of quassia was a specific for cholera—a simon-pure humbug. But this gentleman seized the idea; he cut the skin of the messenger's arm with a lancet so as to draw some blood, and then rubbed in the quassia, telling them what the doctor had said about it. Not a man thus treated died.

The surprising strength and endurance exhibited by lunatics and delirious persons often show that the amount of power which can be commanded by the will under an ordinary stimulant by no means equals the latent strength. Equally true is it that mental and emotional excitement often renders the subject of it unconscious of pain, which otherwise would be unendurable. Even without such excitement, a sudden shock may cause a disease to disappear.

The following was narrated to me by an eminent physician:

I was once called to see a lady, not a regular patient of mine, who had suffered for months with rheumatism. Her situation was desperate, and everything had been done that I could think of except to give her a vapor bath. There was no suitable apparatus, and I was obliged to extemporize it. Finding some old tin pipe, I attached it to the spout of the tea-kettle and then put the other end of the pipe under the bed-clothes, and directed the servant to half fill the kettle, so as to leave room for the vapor to generate and pass through the pipe into the bed. I then sat down to read, and waited for the result. The servant girl, however, desiring to do all she could for her mistress, had filled the kettle to the very lid. Of course there was no room for steam to form, and the hot water—boiling, in fact—ran through the pipe and reached the body of the patient. The instant it struck her she gave a shriek and said, "Doctor, you have scalded me!" and as she said this she leaped out of bed.

"But now," said the physician, "came the wonder. The rheumatism was all gone in that instant, nor did she have any return of it, to my knowledge."

A "MISSING LINK"

IF there were no other, a fatal stumbling-block in the way of the faith-healers is their failure in surgical cases. But they seize everything that could even point at extrahuman interference with the order of nature. The following is taken from the "Provincial Medical Journal" of Leicester and London, June 1, 1886, and is an illustration of the subject:

Another "wonderful cure" at the Bethshan. T. M. N., during a voyage from Liverpool to New York on board the steamship *Helvetia*, sustained a compound fracture of the left humerus at about the line of junction of the middle with the lower third. The injury was treated for a few days by the mercantile surgeon. On his arrival at New York on December 29, 1883 (four days after the accident), he was transferred to a public hospital. He was at once treated, the fracture being fixed in a plaster-of-Paris dressing, and this mode of mechanical fixation was continued for three months, when the surgeon, perceiving no progress toward union, performed the operation of resetting the fractured ends. The arm and forearm were again put in plaster-of-Paris, and retained until his arrival in Liverpool, five months after the date of the injury. On June 10, 1884, he submitted his arm for my inspection, when on removal of the dressing I found there was no attempt at repair, and that the cutaneous wound pertaining to the operation had not healed. The method of treatment I pursued was the following: The forearm was first slung from the neck by its wrist; the ulcer was attended to, and an area inclusive of the fracture partially strangulated by means of india-rubber bands. This was continued for three months, but without appreciable result. I therefore, in addition to this treatment, percussed the site of fracture every three weeks. Four months passed, and yet no change. After seven months the ulceration was healed, and the limb slung as before, partially strangulated and percussed monthly, but, in addition, maintained well fixed by a splint, and carefully readjusted on the occasion when percussion was employed. At length I found evidence

FAITH-HEALING

that repair was progressing, for at this date, December, 1885, it required some force to spring the connection. I now knew it could only be a question of a few weeks for consolidation to be complete, but thought it wise for some little time to leave the arm protected, lest rough usage should destroy the good attained. However, the patient suddenly disappeared, and on the 13th of April I received the following interesting document:

> "No. 2 Woodhouse St., Walton Road,
> "Monday, April 12th.
>
> "Dear Sir: I trust after a very careful perusal of the few following words I may retain the same share of your favorable esteem as previously, and that you will not think too hardly of me because, although I have done a deed which you would not sanction, and which was against your injunctions. Still, I must write and let you know all about it, because I know you have been so kind to me from a purely disinterested motive. I dare say you remember me mentioning the 'faith-healing' some time ago, and to which you remarked that 'it would do no harm to try it, but that you thought I should require *mighty* faith.'
>
> "Well, I have tried it, and I am sure that you will be glad to hear that my arm is not only in my sleeve, but in actual use, and has been for the past three weeks. The pain I bore after the last beating was something dreadful, and being in great trouble at my lodgings at the time, I was downhearted. I was thrown out of my lodgings, and being quite destitute, I reasoned in myself, and came to the conclusion that if I really asked God to make it better right away he would, and I was told that if I would do away with all means and leave it to him, it would be all right. So I just took off all your bandages and splint, and put it in my sleeve. I have now the use of my arm, and it is just the same as my right one — just as strong. Several times I called at your house when on my way to the Bethshan, George's street, but Dr. Gormley slammed me out, and therefore I did not like to come again.
>
> "I cannot describe how thankful I am, doctor, for your past kindness and goodness to me, and that is one reason I have not seen you. I know you will be glad to see me with it in my sleeve. Yours very truly,
> "Tom M. Nicholson.
> "Dr. H. O. Thomas.
> "P. S.— Any communication will reach me if addressed to me at the above, *should you desire to write.*"

There is very little to add to this case. . . . It affords, however, a typical instance of the way a Bethshan thrives. The surgeon tells a patient all but recovered to be cautious lest the results of months of care be nullified, and "fools rush in" and tell him "to dispense with means and all will be well." In this particular instance the result was harmless, but it would be interesting to inquire how many poor deluded victims are consigned to irremediable defects by an ignorant and fanatical display which is a satire upon our civilization.

In this country the case that has been most frequently quoted is narrated by the late W. E. Boardman, who had the story from Dr. Cullis and gives it thus:

The children were jumping off from a bench, and my little son fell and *broke both bones of his arm below the elbow*. My brother, who is a professor of surgery in the college at Chicago, was here on a visit. I asked him to set and dress the arm. He did so; put it in splints, bandages, and in a sling. The dear child was very patient, and went about without a murmur all that day. The next morning he came to me and said, "Dear papa, please take off these things." "Oh, no, my son; you will have to wear these five or six weeks before it will be well!" "Why, papa, it is well." "Oh, no, my dear child; that is impossible!" "Why, papa, you believe in prayer, don't you?" "You know I do, my son." "Well, last night when I went to bed, it hurt me very bad, and I asked Jesus to make it well." I did not like to say a word to chill his faith. A happy thought came. I said, "My dear child, your uncle put the things on, and if they are taken off, he must do it." Away he went to his uncle, who told him he would have to go as he was six or seven weeks, and must be very patient; and when the little fellow told him that Jesus had made him well, he said, "Pooh! pooh! nonsense!" and sent him away. The next morning the poor boy came to me and pleaded with so much sincerity and confidence, that I more than half believed, and went to my brother and said, "Had you not better undo his arm and let him see for himself? Then he will be satisfied. If you do not, I fear, though he is very obedient, he may be tempted to undo it himself, and then it may be worse for him." My brother yielded, took off the bandages and the splints, and exclaimed, "It is well, absolutely well!" and hastened to the door to keep from fainting.

Afterward the Rev. Mr. Gordon introduced the above alleged occurrence into his "Mystery of Healing."

This case was thoroughly investigated by Dr. James Henry Lloyd, of the University of Pennsylvania, and in the "Medical Record" for March 27, 1886, Dr. Lloyd published a letter from the *very child*, who has become a physician.

> DEAR SIR: The case you cite, when robbed of all its sensational surroundings, is as follows: The child was a spoiled youngster who would have his own way; and when he had a *green stick* fracture of the forearm, and, after having had it bandaged for several days, concluded he would much prefer going without a splint, to please the spoiled child the splint was removed, and the arm carefully adjusted in a sling. As a matter of course, the bone soon united, as is customary in children, and being only partially broken, of course all the sooner. This is the miracle.
>
> Some nurse or crank or religious enthusiast, ignorant of matters physiological and histological, evidently started the story, and unfortunately my name — for I am the party — is being circulated in circles of faith-curites, and is given the sort of notoriety I do not crave. . . .
>
> Very respectfully yours,
> CARL H. REED.

EVILS OF THIS SUPERSTITION

MANY well-attested cases of irreparable damage to religion, individuals, and to the peace of churches and families have been placed in my hands or ascertained by investigation. From them I select the following:

> A lady, a member of the Christian church, aged about fifty-five years, had been ailing for two or three years. She fell and bruised her side, and was confined to her bed for some weeks. She was better for a month perhaps, and then the disease developed into internal abscess of the stomach, and she slowly declined until her death, which occurred about five months afterward. She and her family became very anxious for her recovery, and, being very devout, their minds turned to faith-

cures and faith-healers. A month before her death she was in correspondence with one of these persons. This lady appointed an hour in which to pray, and directed that friends in the place where she resided should meet and pray at that time. Her pastor went and prayed. At the close of this interview the patient told him she had received just then a great blessing, so that now she felt reconciled to die, and subsequently said nothing about healing, but much about the heavenly rest which she expected soon to enter. For a long time her nourishment had been, and then was, taken entirely in the form of injections of beef tea. On a certain day a layman who had been healed, and was himself a healer and a prime mover in faith-healing conventions, visited her about noon and stayed until near evening. He told the lady and her children that the Lord had sent him there that she might be instantly healed, read and expounded the book of James, brought out his phial of oil, anointed her forehead, knelt by her bedside, holding her hand in his, and prayed very earnestly for her immediate cure, claiming present conscious testimony by the Holy Spirit that the cure was wrought. On rising from his knees, still holding her hand, he lifted the lady in bed to a sitting posture, and pronounced her cured in the name of the Holy Trinity. A member of the family protested that it was hazardous for her to sit up in that way, as she had not been able to sit up for many weeks. Finally the patient laid down exhausted, and the visitor left, assuring the family that "in four days mother would be up and about." Shortly after this (perhaps an hour) intense pain in the stomach began and kept increasing until the agony became unendurable, so that groans and screams of distress were wrung from her. This continued for twelve hours, when exhaustion and stupor ensued, which lasted until her death, the next day. An autopsy was held by physicians who had been in attendance, and they reported a lesion of the stomach, caused, in their opinion, by the exertion of the patient in arising and sitting up in bed. When our informant met the visiting brother who had had a revelation of the Spirit that the patient was to recover, he inquired after the case, and on being told that our informant was about to go to the funeral, he expressed great surprise and said, "It sometimes happens that way."

Can anything more blasphemous be imagined than the presumptuous claim of a revelation through the

Holy Spirit of a matter of fact, and the pronouncing the dying cured in the name of the Holy Trinity?

Families have been broken up by the doctrine taught in some leading "Faith-Homes" that friends who do not believe this truth are to be separated from because of the weakening effect of their disbelief upon faith. A heartrending letter has reached me from a gentleman whose mother and sister are now residing in a faith-institution of New York, refusing all intercourse with their friends, and neglecting obvious duties of life.

Certain advocates of faith-healing and faith-homes have influenced women to leave their husbands and parents and reside in the homes, and have persuaded them to give thousands of dollars for their purposes, on the ground that "the Lord had need of the money."

This system is connected with every other superstition. The Bible is used as a book of magic. Many open it at random, expecting to be guided by the first passage they see, as Peter was told to open the mouth of the first fish that came up and he would find in it a piece of money. A missionary of high standing with whom I am acquainted was cured of this form of superstition by consulting the Bible on an important matter of Christian duty, and the passage that met his gaze was, "Hell from beneath is moved to meet thee at thy coming." Paganism can produce nothing more superstitious, though many Christians, instead of "searching the Scriptures," still use the Bible as though it were a divining-rod.

It feeds upon impressions, makes great use of dreams and signs, and puts forth statements untrue and pernicious in their influence. A young lady long ill was visited by a minister who prayed with her, in great joy arose from his knees, and said, "Jennie, you are sure to recover. Dismiss all fear.

The Lord has revealed it to me." Soon after, physicians in consultation decided that she had cancer of the stomach, of which she subsequently died. He who had received the impression that she would recover, when met by the pastor of the family, said, "Jennie will certainly get well. The Lord will raise her up. He has revealed it to me." Said the minister, "She has not the nervous disease she had some years ago. The physicians have decided that she has cancer of the stomach." "Oh, well," was the reply, "if that is the case, she is sure to die."

A family living in the city of St. Louis had a daughter who was very ill. They were well acquainted with one of the prominent advocates of faith-healing in the East, who made her case a subject of prayer, and whose wife wrote her a letter declaring that she would certainly be cured, and the Lord had revealed it. The letter arrived in St. Louis one day after her death.

These are cases taken not from the operations of recognized fanatics, but from those of leading lights in this *ignis fatuus* movement.

It is a means of obtaining money under false pretenses. Some who promulgate these views are honest, but underneath their proceedings runs a subtle sophistry. They establish institutions which they call faith-homes, declaring that they are supported entirely by faith, and that they use no means to make their work known or to persuade persons to contribute. Meanwhile they advertise their work and institutions in every possible way, publishing reports in which, though in many instances wanting in business accuracy, they exhibit the most cunning wisdom of the children of this world in the conspicuous publication of letters such as the following:

DEAR BROTHER: The Lord told me to send you fifty dollars for your glorious work. I did so, and have been a great deal happier than I ever was before; and from unexpected quarters *more than three times the amount has come in.*

In one of the papers devoted to this subject this letter recently appeared:

DEAR BROTHER: Please announce through the "Crown of Glory" that I will sail for the western coast of Africa to preach a full salvation in the name of the Lord Jesus Christ, and to heal whomsoever the Lord will by faith, as soon as the Lord sends the balance of the money to pay my fare. I have renounced all rum, wine, cider, tobacco, beer, ale, and medicines — only Jesus! Only Jesus my Savior! I will sail October 10, if the Lord sends the balance of the money to Brother Heller, 48 Orchard st., Newark, N. J. Yours, in Christ,
S. B. MYLER.

A prominent English advocate of this method of raising money, who has done an extraordinary and useful work, on one of his missionary tours in this country explained his curious system with so much eloquence that the founders of certain faith-homes in the United States called upon the editors of various religious papers and endeavored to induce them to set forth that there are institutions in this country conducted on the same principle, naïvely observing that they did not wish his presence and eloquence to divert to England money that should be expended here. Yet they "do not use means"! But as in the case of the supposed faith-healings, for every successful instance there are a large number of unrecorded grievous failures; and many subjects of delusion who have established faith-homes to which the public has not responded have suffered the agonies of death. Some have starved, some have been relieved by benevolent Christian friends, and others have been taken to asylums for the insane. Similar wrecks are to be found all through the land, dazzled and deceived by the careers of the few who have succeeded in getting their enterprises under way and enjoy a monopoly of their limited method of obtaining revenue. Some who succeed are doubtless as sincere men and women as ever lived. Others oscillate between knavery and unbridled fanaticism. The horrible mixture of superstition and blasphemy to which these views frequently lead is not known to all. I quote from a paper published in Newark, N. J., in the interest of faith-healing:

DEATH.—Three of the richest men in Ocean Park, N. J., have died. Faith-healing has been taught in the place, but was rejected by them, so death came.

CHARLESTON, S. C.—A few years ago the Holy Ghost sent me to preach in that city. But they rejected the Gospel and me. A wicked man shot at me and tried to kill me, but God saved me so that I was not harmed. . . . But I had to leave Charleston and do as the great Head of the Church said: . . . "when ye depart out of that house or city, shake off the dust from your feet." Earthquake, September 1, 1886; one-half the city in ruins. It has a population of about fifty thousand people. Ye wicked cities in the world, take warning! God lives!

SUPPOSED DIFFICULTIES

IT has been suggested that if faith-healing can be demonstrated to be subjective, what is called conversion can be accounted for similarly. If by conversion is meant the cataleptic condition which occurred among Congregationalists in the time of Jonathan Edwards, certain Presbyterians and Baptists in the early part of this century in the South and West, and the early Methodists, and is still common among colored people, Second Adventists, and the Salvation Army, and not wholly unknown among others, I admit that such phenomena are of natural origin.

But if conversion is understood to mean a recognition of sinfulness, genuine repentance, and complete trust in the promises of God, accompanied by a controlling determination to live hereafter in obedience to the law of God, this is radically different. Such an experience may be sufficiently intense to produce tears of sorrow or joy, trances, or even lunacy. But neither the lunacy, the trances, nor the tears are essential parts of the conversion. They are results of emotional excitement, differing in individuals according to temperament and education. If these results are believed to have a divine origin—especially when the susceptible are exposed to the contagion of immense crowds swayed by a common impulse and acted upon by oratory—hundreds may succumb to the epidemic who do not experience any moral change, while others who are thus excited may at the same time be genuinely reformed.

The inquiry has been made why these principles do not apply to the miracles of Christ; why I do not sift the evidence in the same way, and explain the facts on the same grounds. What, then, does the New Testament say, and is it rational to believe it?

The first question relates to the issue with the faith-healers. If they performed such works as are recorded of Jesus Christ, a writer professing to believe in his divinity would be compelled to admit their claims to supernatural assistance. But the point made against them is that they do *not* perform works similar to his.

The credibility of the record concerning Christ's works is a question which cannot be raised by Christians, whether they hold the superstitions of the faith-healers or not.

It is conceded that probably no such sifting of the evidence was attempted as can be made of what takes place in this scientific age, that there was a predisposition to accept miracles, and that the ascendancy of religious teachers was maintained largely by the belief of the people in their power to work miracles. To affirm, however, as some do, that there was no investigation, is an exaggeration. The Jews, who did not believe Christ, had every motive to examine the evidence as thoroughly as possible. Still, we possess only the testimony of those who thought they saw. If they beheld and understood, their testimony is conclusive; but standing alone it would be insufficient.

Yet it is rational to accept the record, although we have not the opportunity of seeing the miracles or testing the evidence by scientific methods. A miracle of wisdom may be as convincing as one of physical force. The resurrection from the dead declared of Jesus Christ could not be more contrary to the laws of nature than the conception of such a life and character as his if he never existed. His discourses are as far above human wisdom as his recorded works transcend human power.

The prophecies which the Jews then held and still preserve, taken in connection with their character and history as a nation, afford a powerful presumption of the truth of the narrative. In the ordinary course of human events the death of Christ, after he had made such claims, would have destroyed the confidence of his apostles and scattered them; but their lives were transformed after his death. This is inexplicable unless he appeared again and sustained them by miraculous gifts.

Of the effect of a belief in the teachings of Christ I have had much observation. It convinces me of their truth; for what reforms human nature, developing all that is good, sustaining it in the endeavor to suppress what is evil, supporting it in the difficulties of life, and illuminating death with a loftier hope than life had ever allowed, furnishes evidence of its truth, not in the scientific method, but in a manner equally convincing. Because the record of miraculous facts concerning Christ is inseparably connected with these teachings, it is rational to believe it.

Later ages have had no experience of the ways of God in making special revelations to men; but these things were performed for such a purpose. To allege the experience of modern times against the credibility of extraordinary events *then* appears no less unphilosophical than to bring forward that record in favor of miracles *now*.

Faraday, "the father of modern experimental chemistry," began his celebrated lecture on the Education of the Judgment thus:

> Before entering upon the subject, I must make one distinction, which, however it may appear to others, is to me of the utmost importance. High as man is placed above the creatures around him, there is a higher and far more exalted position within his view; and the ways are infinite in which he occupies his thoughts about the fears or hopes or expectations of a future life. I believe that the truth of that future cannot be brought to his knowledge by any exertion of his mental powers, however exalted they may be; that it is made known to him by other teaching than his own, and is received through simple belief of the testimony given. Let no one suppose for a moment that the self-education I am about to commend in respect of the things of this life extends to any considerations of the hope set before us, as if man by reasoning could find out God. It would be improper here to enter upon this subject further than to claim an absolute distinction between religious and ordinary belief. I shall be reproached with the weakness of refusing to apply those mental operations which I think good in respect of high things to the very highest. I am content to bear the reproach. Yet, even in earthly matters, I believe that the invisible things of him from the creation of the world are clearly seen, being understood by the things that are made, even his eternal power and Godhead; and I have never seen anything incompatible between those things of man which can

be known by the spirit of man which is within him, and those higher things concerning his future which he cannot know by that spirit.

I would not shield myself behind a great name from the charge of inconsistency, but have brought forward this passage because it states, what the life of Faraday illustrated;—the compatibility of intense devotion to the scientific method in its proper sphere, with a full recognition of its limitations, of the value of moral evidence, and of the difference between grounds of belief in nature and revelation.

"CHRISTIAN SCIENCE" AND "MIND CURE"

THIRTY years ago the phrases Christian Science and Mind Cure, in the sense now attached to them, were unknown; to-day in the press, in conversation, in literature, and especially in discussions relating to health and disease, and to the more occult phenomena of human nature, they frequently occur. To many they have no definite meaning, and long conversations are carried on concerning them in which the most diverse views are maintained, ending in confusion and contradiction, because those who converse have not a uniform conception of the signification of the terms. Some declare Christian Science and Mind Cure to be the same; others stoutly deny this, and seek to establish a radical distinction. Some represent Christian Science as a great advance upon ordinary Christianity; others denounce it as but refined Pantheism; while many more brand both Christian Science and Mind Cure as delusion, a reaction from the uncompromising materialism of the age.

Mrs. Mary Baker Glover Eddy, President of the Massachusetts Metaphysical College, claims to have been the first to use the phrase "Christian Science."

It was in Massachusetts, in the year 1866, that I discovered the Science of Metaphysical Healing, which I afterwards named Christian Science. The discovery came to pass in this way.

During twenty years prior to my discovery I had been trying to trace all physical effects to a mental cause; and in January of 1866 I gained the scientific certainty that all causation was Mind, and every effect a mental phenomenon.

Mrs. Eddy further states that about the year 1862 her health was failing rapidly, and she "employed a distinguished mesmerist, Mr. P. P. Quimby—a sensible, elderly gentleman, with some advanced views about healing. . . . There were no Metaphysical Healers then. The Science of Mental Healing had not been discovered."

Whether or not Mrs. Eddy is indebted for her ideas to Mr. Quimby has since been the subject of heated discussion; for the short time which has elapsed since the "discovery" has been long enough for the development of several rival schools, which have engendered toward one another as much intensity of feeling as the *odium theologicum* and *odium medicum* combined. Speaking of her rivals, Mrs. Eddy modestly observes: "Some silly publications, whose only correct or salient points are borrowed, without credit, from 'Science and Health,' would set the world right on Metaphysical Healing, like children thrumming a piano and pretending to teach music or criticise Mozart."

The history of the discovery is of sufficient importance to be given. "The cowardly claim that I am not the originator of my own writings, but that one P. P. Quimby is, has been legally met and punished. . . . Mr. Quimby died in 1865, and my first knowledge of Christian Science, or Metaphysical Healing, was gained in 1866. . . . When he doctored me I was ignorant of the nature of mesmerism, but subsequent knowledge has convinced me that he practiced it."

Mrs. Eddy says that after having been for many years a sufferer from chronic diseases, she met with an accident which produced, according to physicians, a fatal injury. They gave her up to die, and declared that she would not live till noon. She replied that she would be well at that time. Her pastor called after service and found her busy about the house. One of her assistants says that "while she knew that she was healed by the direct and gracious exercise of the divine power, she was indisposed to make an old-time miracle of it."

After three years' meditation she concluded that her recovery was in accordance with general spiritual laws, capable of being known and clearly stated. She then began to teach and write; though prior to the expiration of the three years, namely, in 1867, she taught a purely metaphysical system of healing to, as she says, "the very first student who was ever so instructed since the days of the Apostles and the primitive Church." Her essays were circulated among her students privately. In 1870 she copyrighted her first pamphlet, but did not publish it till six years afterward.

In 1876 she organized the Christian Scientist Association, and in 1879, at a meeting of that association, she organized a Church, "a Mind Healing Church, without creeds, called the Church of Christ." To the pastorate of this she accepted a call, and was ordained in Boston, 1881. The college flourishes, the church has an assistant pastor, and Mrs. Eddy receives so much patronage as a teacher as to compel the publication of the following:

> The authoress takes no patients, and has no time for medical consultation.

Practitioners, who of course are not obliged to waste much time upon such sordid things as anatomy, physiology, or materia medica, are prepared with unusual rapidity. The primary class in Christian Science Mind Healing includes twelve lessons. In the first week six of these are given. The term continues only about three weeks, and the charge for tuition is $300. The normal class requires six lectures. Graduates from the primary class are advised to practise at least one year before entering this class, and for these six lectures they must pay $200. There is also a class of Metaphysical Obstetrics which requires only six lectures, for which $100 must be paid. In addition to these there is a class in Theology, including six lectures on the Scriptures, for which $200 must be paid. The largest discount to an indigent student is $100 on the first course. Husbands and wives, if they enter together the primary class, may pay $300; but, entering at different times, must pay the regular price, and must do that for all other courses, payment being made strictly in advance. It is obvious therefore, that the benefits of the Mind Cure cannot be applied to commercial transactions; and that 800 material dollars, exclusive of board, are required to master the Science of Metaphysical Healing,—unless one were to say that national bank notes are merely material symbols of an immaterial and impalpable essence.

Considering the short time that has elapsed since the "discovery," the number of practitioners, as advertised in one of their magazines, is very large. Sixty-six are women, and twenty-nine men; and all but five of the men appear to be associated with their wives in the practice of the profession. There are also Christian Science institutes and colleges advertised: two in New York, four in Chicago, one in Milwaukee, one in Brooklyn, and one in Colorado. The other institutions do not charge so large a sum as Mrs. Eddy. Some of them agree to give sufficient instruction for $25 to justify the would-be practitioner in beginning. Others communicate all they know, with the privilege of meeting for conversation once a month for a year, on payment of $100. They give diplomas, valued according to the standing of the respective schools. Impostors have arisen, so that Mrs. Eddy has notified the public that all persons claiming to have been her pupils, who cannot show diplomas legally certifying to that effect, are preferring false claims.

THEORY

By a careful examination of the works of those who have written upon this subject, including Evans, Grimké, Stuart, Arens, Taylor, Baldwin, Hazzard, Nichols, Marston, etc., and by conversation with Mental Healers, Christian Scientists, and their patients, I have ascertained that most of them concur with Mrs. Eddy in the fundamental principles of the system, and that where they diverge it is upon minor points.

Her hypothesis is that "the only realities are the Divine Mind and its ideas. . . . That erring mortal views, misnamed *mind*, produce all the organic and animal action of the mortal body. . . . Rightly understood, instead of possessing sentient matter, we have sensationless bodies. . . . Whence came to me this conviction in antagonism to the testimony of the human senses? From the self-evident fact that matter has no sensation; from the common human experience of the falsity of all material things; from the obvious fact that mortal mind is what suffers, feels, sees; since matter cannot suffer."

The method of Mrs. Eddy's reasoning may be seen in the following extracts:

> The ineradicable belief that pain is located in a limb which has been removed, when really the sensation is believed to be in the nerves, is an added proof of the unreliability of physical testimony. . . . Electricity is not a vital fluid, but an element of mortal mind,—the thought-essence that forms the link between what is termed matter and mortal mind. Both are different strata of human belief. The grosser substratum is named *matter*. The more ethereal is called *human mind*, which is the nearer counterfeit of the Immortal Mind, and hence the more accountable and sinful belief. . . . You say, "Toil fatigues me." But what is this *you* or *me* ? Is it muscle or mind ? Which one is tired and so speaks ? Without mind, could the muscles be tired ? Do the muscles talk, or do you talk for them ? Matter is non-intelligent. Mortal mind does the talking, and that which affirms it to be tired first made it so.

Having adopted a theory, she does not shrink from its logical sequences:

> You would not say that a wheel is fatigued; and yet, the body is just as material as the wheel. Setting aside what the human mind says of the body, it would never be weary any more than the inanimate wheel. Understanding this great fact rests you more than hours of repose.

Her most frequently repeated assertions are such as these:

> God is supreme; is mind; is principle, not person; includes all and is reflected by all that is real and eternal; is Spirit, and Spirit is infinite; is the only substance; is the only life. Man was and is the idea of God; therefore mind can never be in man. Divine Science shows that matter and mortal body are the illusions of human belief, which seem to appear and disappear to mortal sense alone. When this belief changes, as in dreams, the material body changes with it, going wherever we wish, and becoming whatsoever belief may decree. Human mortality proves

"CHRISTIAN SCIENCE" AND "MIND CURE"

that error has been engrafted into both the dreams and conclusions of material and mortal humanity. Besiege sickness and death with these principles, and all will disappear.

As these doctrines are unquestionably in substance such as have been held by certain metaphysicians in past ages, Mrs. Eddy feels called upon to answer those who make that charge:

> Those who formerly sneered at it as foolish and eccentric now declare Bishop Berkeley, David Hume, Ralph Waldo Emerson, certain German philosophers, or some unlearned mesmerist, to have been the real originators of Mind Healing. Emerson's ethics are models of their kind; but even that good man and genial philosopher partially lost his mental faculties before his death, showing that he did not understand the Science of Mind Healing, as elaborated in my "Science and Health"; nor did he pretend to do so.

Sickness, then, is a dream of falsity, to be antagonized by the metaphysical healer, mentally, and audibly when it may be necessary.

Mrs. Eddy's theories are her religion, and her Science—so called—is based upon the religious principles which she holds.

One of Mrs. Eddy's former students, named Arens, for whom she entertains a strong spiritual antipathy, has published a volume called "Old Theology in its Application to the Healing of the Sick." In the introduction he writes:

> It will be unnecessary to ask the reader for charitable criticism when I say that I make no claims to being a ripe scholar, and that my knowledge of the English language is very imperfect. The truths set forth in this volume have been expressed as clearly as possible, considering the disadvantages under which I have labored, one of which is the poverty of words in the English language to express spiritual thoughts. It has been found necessary to employ close punctuation, and in some

instances to disregard some rules of grammar and rhetoric, in order to give the requisite shade of thought.

The mental difficulty in understanding him arises from his incompetency as a writer. His reflection upon the poverty of the English language is another form of confessing his ignorance of it; and his disregard of the rules of grammar and rhetoric does not result from his difficulty in giving shades of thought, but from his lack of knowledge of the language. Mrs. Eddy thus described him in 1883:

> When he entered the class of my husband, the late Asa G. Eddy, in 1879, he had no knowledge whatever, and claimed none, as can be shown under his own signature, of Metaphysics or Christian Science. . . . While teaching him my system of Mental Healing, his motives and aims and the general constitution of his mind were found so remote from the requirements of Christian Science, that his teacher despaired of imparting to him a due understanding of the subject. Perhaps it was to meet this great want without remedying it, and cover his lack of learning, that he committed to memory many paragraphs from my works, and is in the habit of repeating them in his attempts to lecture. He, who now proclaims himself a professor in the solemn department that he assumes as a jay in borrowed plumes, was the most ignorant and empty-minded scholar I ever remember of examining.

That his earlier work consists largely of passages taken from Mrs. Eddy's writings, and that it is as a whole in every respect inferior to them, is the simple statement of a fact. He has, however, acquired considerable reputation, and has a constituency. Before advancing the fundamental principles of his system, he attempts to show the inconsistencies of medical science in the following passage:

> Materia medica teaches that mercury cures, also that mercury kills; that ipecac causes vomiting, and that an overdose

checks it, etc.; these are contradictions in themselves. A rule that can be contradicted is not demonstrable, and therefore not truth. If one and one made two only occasionally, and at other times made three or more, it would be no fact or rule, because not demonstrable, and no dependence could be placed upon it. If from a science (truth) it is found that mercury cures, it would be found that the more of that so-called necessary quality taken into the system, the better it would be for the patient; such would be the result from a perfect rule or from truth.

Here is an example of his style:

Suppose I should be walking past a house, and a pane of glass should fall from an upper window cutting me and causing my death; the glass was made and placed by life, and life broke it and caused it to fall. My life brought me here from Prussia and carried me by the house at the time that happened; therefore life was the cause of my death, and, strange as it may seem, is the cause of all action.

From this profound (?) reasoning he concludes:

If life is the cause of all action it must be the cause of sickness. . . . Thought is the first product of life, and as the thought is so will the action be. Life cannot act contrary to the thoughts which are become beliefs or opinions, that is, which have taken root or are become attached to it, unless it acts unconsciously.

Mrs. Eddy sued this Dr. Arens for infringing her copyright, and obtained judgment against him, so that he was compelled to destroy a large edition of one of his pamphlets.

Dr. Arens established a university in the city of Boston, incorporated five or six years, called the "University of the Science of Spirit." It confers the following degrees: "F. D.," Defender of the Faith, and "S. S. D.," Doctor of the Science of Spirit. The charge for instruction in the general course is one hundred dollars. These courses are somewhat pretentious. The first treats the "Scientific Basis of Theology," "the Difference between God and the Universe," etc., and, proceeding through twenty-one theological points, concludes by setting forth "the First Step in Immortality," and "How to Destroy Sickness." The second course discusses "Theos, Chaos, and Cosmos"; gives a theory of the creation of the universe down to the creation of the "first material human body," which it treats under "its outline and quality; the necessity for respiration; the first consciousness of existence; the separation of male and female; the origin of self-will and its results." And finally, "the beginning of sickness and trouble."

Dr. Marston treats "God, Man, Matter, Disease, Sin, and Death, Healing, Treatment, and Universal Truth." In his book he states that "the mental healer does not care by what medical name the distress is known; it may be nervousness, dyspepsia, asthma, fever,—words all alike to him, since the effects they denote are simply reflections or registers of wrong thinking." In illustrating this he says:

A case may be cited to illustrate the meaning: A middle-aged man who has suffered many years with chronic rheumatism, until it is torture for him to move, has also an excitable temper, a despotic will, and is so intolerant that he cannot abide opposition, but flies into a towering rage if he is crossed. He has had many physicians who ascribe the painful inflammation of his joints to an improper secretion of uric acid; and his nervousness and irritability are easily accounted for by the prolonged suffering he has endured. This case presents the same conditions to the mental healer, but his conclusions are different. To him the bodily trouble is a reflection or effect of lack of mental ease; and the unamiable nature results from a dominant feeling that other people are enemies seeking to oppose the poor man's wishes and thwart his plans. In treating the case, the doctor addresses remedies to the disturbed secretions which are an effect, while the mental healer directs his to the primary cause, which is fear.

"CHRISTIAN SCIENCE" AND "MIND CURE"

His cure is reduced to its simplest form as follows: "The senses say matter can suffer pain; God says matter is insensible. The senses declare a man sick; God says the real man knows nothing of disease." Under the head of Sin and Death he says: "Scientific Christianity does not recognize the definition of theology, but holds that, strictly speaking, there is no sin." He finally describes the cure thus: "A mental cure is the discovery made by a sick person that he is well."

W. F. Evans, a voluminous writer, formerly an evangelical minister, then a Swedenborgian, and lately a mental healer, remarks:

> The process is essentially a spiritual work; *it is held that there is a part of us that is never sick, and this part is mentally worked upon so as to control the sick person's consciousness, this destroys the sickness,* for mind cures matter. A disciple of this school is sick—no, he is not sick, for that is something which he will not admit; he has a belief that he is sick; he then says mentally to the rebellious body, "What are you? You have no power over me; you are merely the covering given to me for present purposes; it is an error to suppose that I am sick; I recognize the great truth that I myself, my individuality, my personality, my mind, cannot be sick, for it is immortal, made in the image of God; when I recognize the existence of that truth there is no room left for the existence of error; two things cannot occupy one and the same place; error cannot exist in the same place with truth, therefore error is not in existence; hence I am not sick."

Mrs. Grimké, author of "Personified Unthinkables," says:

> Now, rheumatism or pneumonia, etc., are *verbal* expressions for unthinkables, just as $2+2=5$ is a verbal expression for a lie. By means of the picturing faculty, both of the individual and of those about him, the outward manifestation of the unthinkable will express itself upon the body just as surely as the magic-lantern will reflect the picture inserted between the light

and the lenses when the proper conditions are met. . . .
The problem of Health, then, would be how to cultivate and keep clean and healthy pictures in the mind. Health would then be an essential part of the ego. Man would be a strict unity, not a trinity, of Intellect, Body, and Morals, and the absolutely necessary postulates of this *Unity* would be Infinite Mind, Freedom, and Eternal Life.

There are those who in their own opinion have reached a greater elevation than either the Christian Scientists or the Mind Curers, "and profess to heal by the transfer of psychic energy." The chief practitioner in this sphere informed me that the relative rank of these sciences is, 1. The lower grade—the mere physical system. 2. What is called animal magnetism. 3. The mind cure. 4. The spirits (when they are good spirits). 5. Including all that is good in the others, he places in the *supernal*. He claimed that there has been in all ages an order called the *Inspirati*, who practised this method, and offered to make me a Knight of that order.

This will suffice until it fails to attract patients, when, no doubt, a sixth order, that of the *Empyrean*, will be devised.

Some of the Christian Scientists have attempted to construct a technical language, which, when translated, shows that they attach as much importance to learned terms as does any form of the material science that they denounce. "Gnosis.—The 'Spiritual Understanding,' the 'Immediate Intuition.' VIR.—The God in Man. HARMATIA.—Off-the-trackness. HOMO.—The Creature of God. EGO.—The Homo *as he is.* NEMO.—The Homo as he sees himself. ENTHEASM.—Direct Communication with God. NIHILOID.—Like unto nothing, the proper name of disease, disorder, discomfort. YOGA.—Concentration of Thought. DAMA.—Subjugation of Sense. KARMA.—Law of

Cause and Effect. MAYA.—Illusion, 'Mortal Mind,' False Beliefs.—Chaos, The *Habitat* of Humbug."

Most of these terms appear to have had an oriental origin, and are as valuable in affecting the ordinary mind as chloride of sodium for salt, capsicum for pepper, and H_2O for water. They serve also to make it appear that the Science is difficult, and that large fees for instruction are reasonable.

They make use of certain forms of expression which savor more strongly of cant than any phrases that have ever been used by religious sects. They use the word "belief" in speaking of a disease, or even of a defect of character. A lady, talking with a practitioner of this school of a mutual acquaintance, said she thought her selfish. "Yes," replied the Christian Scientist, "I believe she has a strong belief in selfishness."

To a patient who had every symptom of a torpid liver another healer of the school said, "It is unfortunate that you have such a belief in bile." To which the astonished patient, new to the Science, replied that he thought any one would have the same belief who had the same kind of liver.

PRACTICE

THE manner in which Christian Science antagonizes dreams of falsity is interesting, whether the theories be accepted or not.

First.—Both the patient and the metaphysical healer must be taught that

Anatomy, Physiology, Treatises on Health, sustained by what is termed material law, are the husbandmen of sickness and disease. It is proverbial that as long as you read medical works you will be sick. . . . Clairvoyants and medical charlatans are the prolific sources of sickness. . . . They first help to form the image of illness in mortal minds, by telling patients that they have a disease; and then they go to work to destroy that disease. They unweave their own webs. . . . When there were fewer doctors, and less thought was given to sanitary subjects, there were better constitutions and less disease.

Second.—Diet is a matter of no importance.

We are told that the simple food our forefathers ate assisted to make them healthy; but that is a mistake. Their diet would not cure dyspepsia at this period. With rules of health in the head, and the most digestible food in the stomach, there would still be dyspeptics.

Third.—Exercise is of no importance.

Because the muscles of the blacksmith's arm are strongly developed, it does not follow that exercise did it, or that an arm less used must be fragile. If matter were the cause of action, and muscles, without the coöperation of mortal mind, could lift the hammer and smite the nail, it might be thought true that hammering enlarges the muscles. But the trip-hammer is not increased in size by exercise. Why not, since muscles are as material as wood and iron?

Fourth.—A proper view of Mrs. Eddy's publications is, however, of great importance.

My publications alone heal more sickness than an unconscientious student can begin to reach. If patients seem the worse for reading my book, this change may either arise from the frightened mind of the physician, or mark the crisis of the disease. Perseverance in its perusal would heal them completely.

Fifth.

Never tell the sick they have more courage than strength. Tell them rather that their strength is in proportion to their courage. . . . Instruct the sick that they are not helpless victims; but that, if they only know how, they can resist disease and ward it off, just as positively as they can a temptation to sin.

Sixth.—In preparing to treat patients, the healer must strengthen and steady his own mind.

Be firm in your understanding that Mind governs the body. Have no foolish fears that matter governs, and can ache, swell, and be inflamed from a law of its own; when it is self-evident that matter can have no pain or inflammation. . . . If you believe in inflamed or weak nerves, you are liable to an attack from that source. You will call it neuralgia, but I call it Illusion. . . . When treating the sick, first make your mental plea in behalf of harmony, . . . then realize the absence of disease. . . . Use such powerful eloquence as a Congressman would employ to defeat the passage of an inhuman law.

Seventh.—You are fortunate if your patient knows little or nothing, for "a patient thoroughly booked in medical theories has less sense of the divine power, and is more difficult to heal through Mind, than an aboriginal Indian who never bowed the knee to the Baal of civilization."

Eighth.—See that the "minds which surround your patient do not act against your influence by continually expressing such opinions as may alarm or discourage. . . . You should seek to be alone with the sick while treating them."

Ninth.—Bathing and rubbing are of no use.

Bathing and rubbing to alter the secretions, or remove unhealthy exhalations from the cuticle, receive a useful rebuke from Christian Healing. . . . John Quincy Adams presents an instance of firm health and an adherence to hygienic rules, but there are few others.

Tenth.—What if the patient grow worse?

Suppose the patient should appear to grow worse. This I term *chemicalization*. It is the upheaval produced when Immortal Truth is destroying erroneous and mortal belief. Chemicalization brings sin and sickness to the surface, as in a fermenting fluid, allowing impurities to pass away. Patients unfamiliar with the cause of this commotion, and ignorant that it is a favorable omen, may be alarmed. If such is the case, explain to them the law of this action.

Eleventh.—Subtle mental practices are recommended.

I will here state a phenomenon which I have observed. If you call mentally and silently the disease by name, as you argue against it, as a general rule the body will respond more quickly; just as a person replies more readily when his name is spoken; but this is because you are not perfectly attuned to Divine Science, and need the arguments of truth for reminders. To let Spirit bear witness without words is the more scientific way.

This is further modified:

You may call the disease by name when you address it mentally; but by naming it *audibly*, you are liable to impress it upon the mind. The Silence of Science is eloquent and powerful to unclasp the hand of disease and reduce it to nothingness.

Twelfth.—Some of the things that are *not* to be done.

A Christian Scientist never gives medicine, never recommends hygiene, never manipulates. He never tries to "focus mind." He never places patient and practitioner "back to back," never consults "spirits," nor requires the life history of his patient. Above all, he cannot trespass on the rights of Mind through animal magnetism.

The foregoing rules for practice are taken from Mrs. Eddy's different works.

The difference between the views of Mrs. Eddy and those who diverge from her is superficial, though neither she nor they will admit it. Miss Kate Tay-

"CHRISTIAN SCIENCE" AND "MIND CURE" 81

lor, in "Selfhood Lost in Godhood," referring to Mrs. Eddy's large work, says: "It can be read with profit by any who are seeking truth with sincerity, and with no tendency to become biased." She also says that she was formerly a member of the Christian Science Association, and "learned that limitations are not conducive to growth, and that, as Emerson truly says, 'God always disappoints monopolies,'" and frankly gives her opinion of those denounced by her former preceptor.

The so-called mal-practitioners and mesmerists therein mentioned, on thorough investigation,—not only by myself, but in company with others who seek to be liberal-minded and to give Truth its due wherever it exists,—I find to be simply those who have separated themselves from the Association, that they might pursue their own convictions of right, and step out of the regular ranks of stereotyped terms to let their thoughts find expression in their own words.

The chief point of departure in Miss Taylor's theories from those of Mrs. Eddy is in the value attached to a knowledge of the preceding life of the patient.

Physical disease has many different causes. The physician treating a patient is often narrowed in his efforts to do good, because of some hidden moral or mental cause, some underlying fear, some sorrow, some inherited proclivity, some wrong unforgiven, some trait of character, some past occurrence which has tinged, perhaps almost unconsciously, the whole tenor of a life. It is not necessary that a person's innermost sacred thoughts and life be unveiled, as the physician does not expect, neither does he like, to receive confidences, unless, indeed, they are given voluntarily with a feeling of trust. Some word or hint, though, to the physician would often aid materially. . . . The treatment consists in a vigorous holding of the patient to his right of soul-growth, unobstructed and unretarded by physical defects. . . . In answer to the question, "Is it prayer?" I would first quote Victor Hugo's definition of prayer,—"Every thought is a prayer; there are moments when, whatever be the attitude of the body, the soul is on its knees,"—

and then answer, Yes, it *is* prayer. *Prayer* with the old interpretation begs the Father to change the unchangeable, while *prayer* with the new interpretation lifts the beggar to a comprehension that he himself has omitted to take the gifts already prepared for him from the foundation of the world.

She gives this advice to the sick:

Eradicate all thoughts of physiology, drugs, laws of health, sickness, and pain, and know that God is the only panacea,—divine love the only medicine. . . . Seek the help of a Christian Healer. . . . Judge him not unjustly, . . . neither be in opposition, for his is a good motive. . . . While under his treatment obey any natural impulse, without fear of consequence. Remember! without fear. This does not mean to be foolhardy in the beginning,—unless the cure should be almost instantaneous,—but advance gradually. . . . If you have a time during the treatment when you should feel worse, do not be discouraged. . . . Look forward. . . . One little secret it is well to know. . . . Deny every thought of sickness every time it enters your mind. . . . Never use will-power, mistaking it for divine Truth.

Also Mrs. Stuart teaches the importance of a knowledge of the previous life:

A man came to me from Erie, Penn., with what was called by different M. D's softening of the brain and Bright's disease of the kidneys. After questioning him I found his trouble dated back to the Chicago fire. Now he was not conscious of any fear, was in no personal danger for himself or family. But he was in that atmosphere of mental confusion and terror all through the city. He was cured by treatment on that point and nothing else. A woman came to me who had suffered five years with what the doctors called rheumatism. I happened to know that the death of a child had caused this effect. By silently erasing that picture of death and holding in its place an image of Life, eternal Life, she was entirely cured in twenty minutes.

SPECIMEN TREATMENTS

MENTAL treatment is that which the metaphysical healer is supposed to be giving the patient when she sits silently before him for a period longer or shorter according to her judgment of the necessities of the case. Some of the practitioners have revealed the thoughts which constitute a mental treatment, so that if truth is an element of their system, we can speak confidently upon this part of it.

> I said to him mentally: "You have no disease; what you call your disease is a fixed mode of thought arising from the absence of positive belief in absolute good. Be stronger," I said, "you must believe in absolute good; I am looking at you, and I see you a beautiful, strong spirit, perfectly sound. What makes you think yourself diseased? You are not diseased; the shadow of a doubt is reflected on your feet, but it has no real existence. There, look down yourself and see that it is gone. Why, it was a mere negation, and the place where you located it now shows for itself as sound as the rest of your body. Don't you know that imperfection is impossible to that beautiful creature, your real self? Since there is no evil in all the universe, and since man is the highest expression of good amidst ubiquitous Good, how can you be diseased? You are not diseased. There is not an angel in all the spheres sounder or more divine than you." Then I spoke out aloud: "There now," I said, "you won't have that pain again." *As I said it there was a surge of conviction through me that seemed to act on the bloodvessels of my body and made me tingle all over."*—HELEN WILMANS.

To this treatment I shall refer in elucidating the causes of the phenomena.

Dr. Evans controverts some of Mrs. Eddy's theories:

> To modify a patient's thinking in regard to himself and his disease, we employ the principle of suggestion or positive

affirmation—not mental argument, as it is sometimes called, for argument creates doubt and reaction. No sick man was ever cured by reasoning with him, mentally or verbally. It is the business of the man who *knows* the truth, not to argue, but to *affirm*. . . . No *intelligent* practitioner of the mind cure will ignore wholly all medical science. . . . The phrenopathic system is not necessarily antagonistic to other methods of cure, as the various hygienic regulations, and even the use of the harmless specific remedies.

He repudiates Mrs. Eddy's ideas about the personality of God, and says:

It is not necessary to deny the personality of God. . . . Neither is it necessary to deny the personality and persistent individuality of the human spirit.

He also flatly denies Miss Taylor's theories, saying, "The selfhood is not lost in Godhood." "It is not necessary to tell a man dying of consumption that he is not sick, for that is not true." He says that one may or may not use the imposition of hands in healing the sick.

As an example of Christian Science superstition exceeding anything attempted by the most ignorant advocates of patent Faith Healing, read the following, taken *verbatim*, italics, small caps, etc., from a text-book on Mind Cure, issued by the President of the "New York School of Primitive and Practical Christian Science," who states that *his* school will be free from "eccentricity, pretension, and fanaticism"!

PRAYER FOR A DYSPEPTIC.

Holy Reality! We BELIEVE in Thee that Thou art EVERYWHERE present. We *really* believe it. Blessed Reality we do not pretend to believe, think we believe, believe that we believe. WE BELIEVE. Believing that Thou art every where present, we believe that Thou art in this patient's stomach, in every fibre, in every cell, in every atom, that Thou are the sole, only Reality of that stomach. Heavenly, Holy Reality, we *will* try not to be such hypocrites and infidels, as every day of our lives to affirm our faith in Thee and then immediately begin to tell how sick we are, forgetting that Thou art everything and that Thou art not sick, and therefore that nothing in this universe was ever sick, is now sick, or can be sick. Forgive us our sins in that we have this day talked about our backaches, that we have told our neighbors that our food hurts us, that we mentioned to a visitor that there was a lump in our stomach, that we have wasted our valuable time which should have been spent in Thy service, in worrying for fear that our stomach would grow worse, in that we have disobeyed Thy blessed law in thinking that some kind of medicine would help us. We know, Father and Mother of us all, that there is no such a thing as a really diseased stomach, that the disease is the Carnal Mortal Mind given over to the World, the Flesh, and the Devil; that the mortal mind is a twist, a distortion, a false attitude, the HARMATIA of Thought. Shining and Glorious Verity, we recognize the great and splendid FACT that the moment we really believe the Truth, Disease ceases to trouble us, that the Truth is that there is no Disease in either *real* Body or Mind; that in the Mind what *seems* to be a *disease* is a False Belief, a Parasite, a hateful Excrescence, and that what happens in the Body is the shadow of the LIE in the Soul. Lord, help us to believe that ALL Evil is Utterly Unreal; that it is silly to be sick, absurd to be ailing, wicked to be wailing, atheism and denial of God to say "I am sick." Help us to stoutly affirm with our hand in Your hand, with our eyes fixed on Thee that we have no Dyspepsia, that we never had Dyspepsia, that we will never have Dyspepsia, that there is no such thing, that there never was any such thing, that there never will be any such thing. Amen.—HAZZARD.

It is claimed by all the Christian Science and Mind Cure practitioners that they can operate upon patients *at a distance.*

There is no space nor time to mind. A person in St. Louis may be near to me while I am in New York. A person in the same room may be very distant. Sit down and think about the person you wish to affect. Think long enough and strong enough and you are sure to reach him.—HAZZARD.

The following is a case of heart disease which I cured without having seen the patient: "Please find enclosed a check for five hundred dollars, in reward for your services that can never be repaid. The day you received my husband's letter I became conscious for the first time in forty-eight hours. My servant brought my wrapper, and I arose from bed and sat up. . . . The enlargement of my left side is all gone, and the doctors pronounce me rid of heart disease. I had been afflicted with it from infancy. It became organic enlargement of the heart and dropsy of the chest. I was only waiting and almost longing to die, but you have healed me. How wonderful to think of it, when you and I have never seen each other."—EDDY.

One of them says:

Remember that every thought that you think will be transferred to the persons thought of if you think long enough and strong enough.—HAZZARD.

This surpasses the love-powders that are sold among the colored people and the ignorant, as it is necessary to purchase and administer them, which is sometimes considerable trouble.

The practical directions to attain this power are as follows:

How to "concentrate." 1. Look at an object on the ceiling ten minutes; think of that object alone. 2. Write a proposition on a sheet of paper, as "God is the only reality." Think it for ten minutes with your eyes fixed upon the paper. 3. Begin to think of a subject, and give a dollar to the poor for every time your mind wanders. How to "subjugate." Forget yourself, forget the world, forget you have a body, forget you have any business or friends. Empty your mind of its contents. Be a man of one idea. Get out of yourself.—HAZZARD.

The rules for absent treatment are:

1. Seat yourself alone. Let the room be silent. 2. Subjugate your senses to all else but your thought. 3. Fix your thought upon the patient. 4. Picture him in your mind. 5. Go through the treatment.—HAZZARD.

The patient may be in three different ways. He may be sympathetic; that will help you greatly. He may be apathetic; that is not so good, but better than the next. He may be antipathetic, hostile; then say not a word, but *silently* "give it to him" till he becomes less "cantankerous" and more Christlike.—HAZZARD.

MIND CURERS *versus* FAITH HEALERS, MESMERISTS, ETC.

MRS. EDDY speaks of Mesmerism in this way:

Mortal mind, acting from the basis of sensuous belief in matter, is animal magnetism. . . . In proportion as you understand Christian Science you lose animal magnetism. . . . Its basis being a belief and this belief an error, animal magnetism, or mesmerism, is a mere negation, possessing neither intelligence nor power. . . . An evil mind at work mesmerically is an engine of mischief little understood. . . . Animal magnetism, clairvoyance, mediumship, and mesmerism are antagonistic to this Science, and would prevent the demonstration thereof. . . . The Mesmeriser produces pain by making his subjects believe that he feels it; here pain is proved to be a belief without any adequate cause. That social curse, the mesmerist, by making his victims believe they cannot move a limb, renders it impossible for them to do so until their belief or understanding masters his.

Of Spiritualism:

Spiritualism with its material accompaniments would destroy the supremacy of Spirit.

And of Clairvoyance specifically:

Clairvoyance investigates and influences mortal thought only. . . . Clairvoyance can do evil, can accuse wrongfully, and err in every direction.

Of Faith Cure:

It is asked, Why are faith cures sometimes more speedy than some of the cures wrought through Christian Scientists? Because faith is belief, and not understanding; and it is easier to believe than to understand Spiritual Truth. It demands less cross-bearing, self-renunciation, and Divine Science, to admit the claims of the personal senses, and appeal for relief to a humanized God, than to deny those claims and learn the divine way, drinking his cup, being baptized with his baptism, gaining the end through persecution and purity. Millions are believing in God, or Good, without sharing the fruits of goodness, not having reached its Science. Belief is mental blindness, if it admits Truth without understanding it. It cannot say with the Apostle, "I know in whom I have believed." There is even danger in the mental state called belief, for if Truth is admitted but not understood, error may enter through this same channel of ignorance. The Faith cure has devout followers, whose Christian practice is far in advance of mere theory.

Marston, speaking of change in the inverted thought of the sick person, says:

Since a change of the inverted thought of the sick person is all that can be produced by extraneous influence, the treatment of a professional Healer is not the only means of securing it. While a majority of cases are affected in that way, there are well-attested instances to show that anything that will enable the sick person to change his thought may put him in a condition to receive spiritual healing. A text from Scripture or some other writings may be brought to his mind with such force as to do this, or some sudden event may startle him out of his chronic delusion. It is in this way alone that we can account for cures that seem to result from prayer, a resort to relics, charms, and other things believed to possess peculiar virtue. This is why good results follow any one of the thousand absurd acts, by the performance of which superstitious and credulous people seek to be restored to health.

Another remarks:

The question is often asked, In what does the Christian Science healing differ from the faith cure? In the faith cure the patient must have faith; in Christian Science that is not necessary; patients have frequently been helped or entirely cured, without knowing they were being treated. . . . No great

"CHRISTIAN SCIENCE" AND "MIND CURE"

faith is necessary on the part of the patient; but it will expedite his recovery if he take interest enough in the method by which he is being healed to read suitable books on the subject, and converse profitably with the healer. . . . Prayer to a personal God affects the sick like a drug that has no efficacy of its own, but borrows its power from human faith and belief. The drug does nothing because it has no intelligence.

TESTS OF THE THEORY

First Test. If their principles be true, food should not be necessary. Mrs. Eddy affirms this:

> Gustatory pleasure is a sensuous illusion, an illusion that diminishes as we understand our spiritual being and ascend the ladder of Life. This woman learned that food neither strengthens nor weakens the body,—that mind alone does this. . . . Teach them that their bodies are nourished more by Truth than by food.

Then, finding herself unable to silence the testimony of the senses, she endeavors to circumvent it thus:

> Admitting the common hypothesis, that food is requisite to sustain human life, there follows the necessity for another admission, in the opposite direction,—namely, that food has power to destroy life, through its deficiency or excess, in quality or quantity. This is a specimen of the ambiguous character of all material health-theories. They are self-contradictory and self-destructive,—"a kingdom divided against itself, that is brought to desolation." If food preserves life, it cannot destroy it. The truth is, food does not affect the life of man; and this becomes self-evident when we learn that God is our only life. Because sin and sickness are not qualities of Soul or Life, we have hope in immortality; but it would be foolish to venture beyond our present understanding, foolish to stop eating, until we gain more goodness and a clearer comprehension of the living God. In that perfect day of understanding, we shall neither eat to live, nor live to eat.

When they dispense with food because "mortal mind" is under the influence of an illusion concerning it, — absurdly supposing "that food supports life," — and continue to live with the accidents of the human body sustained entirely by the divine "substance" of which they speak, they will furnish a demonstration which will utterly destroy every remaining illusion of mortal mind. But so long as they eat, they are either voluntarily perpetuating an illusion, or demonstrating that they are wrong in their notions. If they are in such a low stage as to be compelled to eat when it would not be necessary if they were in a higher plane, they may, for the same reason, be compelled to use drugs.

Second Test. They deny that drugs, *per se*, as taken into the human system, have any power.

> Christian Science divests material drugs of their imaginary power. . . . The uselessness of drugs, the emptiness of knowledge, the nothingness of matter and its imaginary laws, are apparent as we rise from the rubbish of belief to the acquisition and demonstration of spiritual understanding. . . . When the sick recover by the use of drugs, it is the law of a general belief, culminating in individual faith that heals, and according to this faith will the effect be. — EDDY.

Surely the mind needs healing that could invent the following absurdity:

> The not uncommon notion that drugs possess absolute, inherent curative virtues of their own involves an error. Arnica, quinine, opium, could not produce the effects ascribed to them except by imputed virtue. Men think they will act thus on the physical system, consequently they do. The property of alcohol is to intoxicate; but if the common thought had endowed it simply with a nourishing quality like milk, it would produce a similar effect. A curious question arises about the origin of healing virtues, if it be admitted that all drugs were originally destitute of them. We can conceive of a time in the mental

history of the race when no therapeutic value was assigned to certain drugs, when, in fact, it was not known that they possessed any. How did it come to pass that common thought, or any thought, endowed them with healing virtue, in the first place? Simply in this way: Man finding himself unprotected, and liable to be hurt by the elements in the midst of which he lived, forgot the true source of healing, and began to seek earnestly for material remedies for disease and wounds. The desire for something led to experiments; and with each trial there was associated the hope that the means applied would prove efficacious. Then what was at first an earnest hope came at length to be a belief; and thus, by gradual steps, a belief in the contents of the entire pharmacopœia was established.— MARSTON.

It is true that in many cases the effect of a medicine is to be attributed entirely to the imagination, or to the belief that it will have such and such effects; but the statement of such extreme positions as these shows the irrationality of the theories upon which they are based. According to the above, if it were generally believed that alcohol were unintoxicating, nourishing, and bland as milk, it would be an excellent article with which to nourish infants; and, on the other hand, if it were generally believed that milk were intoxicating, all the influences of alcohol would be produced upon those who drank it. If the public could only be educated to believe alcohol to be nourishing, the entire mammalian genus might be nursing their offspring upon alcohol with equally good results. No insane asylum can furnish a more transparent delusion.

That drugs produce effects upon animals has been demonstrated beyond the possibility of contradiction, and that, when the animals did not know that they were taking drugs; and small doses have produced not the slightest effect, while large doses—the animals in each case not knowing that they were taking medicines—have produced great effect, and do so with uniformity. Also the effect of medicines upon idiots and unconscious infants is capable of exact demonstration.

Allied to the effect of drugs is that of *poisons*, almost every drug having the effect of a poison if taken in excess. Some poisons, however, are of such nature that the smallest possible dose may be attended with fatal results. In the case of animals, poisons introduced into the system without the knowledge of the animals do their work effectually. Strychnine carefully introduced into a piece of meat so small that a cat will swallow it whole, will in a very short time show its effects. The instinct of the animal will cause its rejection if there be the slightest possibility of perceiving it; but if sufficient means be taken to keep the animal from knowing that it is taking anything except meat, it will swallow the meat, and the poison will do its work.

These facts are admitted by the advocates of Christian Science and Mind Cure, and the absolute lunacy of their theories is seen in the manner in which they attempt to account for the effects.

» If a dose of poison is swallowed through mistake, the patient dies, while physician and patient are expecting favorable results. Did belief cause this death? Even so, and as directly as if the poison had been intentionally taken. . . . The few who think a drug harmless, where a mistake has been made in the prescription, are unequal to the many who have named it poison, and so the majority opinion governs the result.—EDDY.

It is said that arsenic kills; but it would be very difficult for any one to prove how it kills; since persons have had all the symptoms of arsenic poisoning without having taken any arsenic; and again, persons have taken arsenic and did not die. . . . Suppose you take a child that knows nothing about arsenic, and administer the usual dose, the child will probably die, but I will show you that the arsenic was not the cause of the death. . . . Here you may say, "What had the life of the child to do with the action, the child not knowing anything about arsenic?" We will admit that the child was ignorant of the nature of the poison, but all who are educated in physiology and materia medica know that it kills, therefore the thought, although unconscious to the child, was hereditary in its life. It is, indeed, a universal thought admitted as a fact in every life or soul. A thought is a product of life and is action, and this thought, produced and accepted by life, acts upon the life of the child and produces unconsciously a confusion therein. This confusion produces a fear; this fear in the child's life heats the blood and causes the first conscious action.—ARENS.

The effects of various experiments, with chemicals and medicine, upon cats and dogs, are studied most minutely by distinguished scientific men, and the results witnessed published to the world with a presumption of wisdom and profundity of learning that carry the conviction to most minds that the properties of such drugs, and their effects upon the *human system*, have been forever established. And Materia Medica falls back upon these so-called demonstrations of Science as absolutely indisputable proofs of its Theories. Now it never seems to have occurred to them that all the effects witnessed of such experimenting might be accounted for on the basis of *Thought*, and with the view of investigating the subject to establish a totally opposite explanation; and to show that Mind acting on Matter could account for all their facts, the following experiments have been recently made: The object of the experiments was a dog, a noble thoroughbred, of great sagacity and intelligence. The first experiment consisted in conveying commands to him entirely through *mind*. Not a word was *spoken*, but his mistress would say to him *mentally*,—"Carlo, come here," or "Carlo, lie down," and although the *thought* might have to be repeated mentally a number of times, yet it would reach him, and sometimes he would respond almost immediately. Second experiment: One day his master discovered an appearance to which he gave the name *Mange*. All the dogs around were having it. It was catching,—Dr. So-and-So had pronounced it mange, and prescribed a mixture of Sulphur and Castor Oil, etc., which was to be applied *externally* in such a way that Carlo, in attempting to remove the preparation with his tongue, would get a dose into his system. But here the mistress interposed, and insisted that Carlo should be subjected wholly to mental treatment. The result was entirely satisfactory. The appearance vanished as it came. Again the experiment of placing Carlo entirely under the intelligence of his master's mind and thoughts for a certain period was tried, and compared with the effects of leaving him wholly under his mistress's mind. In the former case he soon exhibited every symptom of dyspepsia and indigestion in every form to which the master was subject, and in a very marked degree. But under the thought of the mistress, every symptom and appearance vanished at once. He soon attained a perfection of physical condition which constantly attracted the notice of every one. Experiments of this kind were carried much further, and can be by any one who wishes to test the matter for themselves. In all the instances just mentioned, the physical condition of the dog responded to the mind under whose influence it chanced to be. Love and Fear (*especially fear*) are the most marked characteristics of the animal mind. The instances are innumerable where the instinct of the animal surpasses the reason of man in detecting the kindly thought, or the thought of *harm*, toward itself. When a scientific experimenter gives a drug to a dog, it is done with a perfect certainty in his mind that disorder, derangement of the system, suffering, etc., in some form or another, are sure to follow. A *fear* corresponding to the thought of the man instantly seizes upon the dog, and various results *do* follow. The experimenter notes them down and then proceeds to try his drug on dog number 2, all the while holding in his mind an image of the results of experiment number 1, expecting to see similar results. In all probability he sees them.—STUART.[1]

Third Test. Extraordinary accidents to the body. Whatever may be said of the power of thought in the production of ordinary disease, the effects of accidents to persons who are entirely unconscious when

[1] Mrs. Stuart in the foregoing passage is only a little more absurd than Mrs. Eddy. "The preference of mortal mind for any method creates a demand for it, and the body seems to require it. You can even educate a healthy horse so far in physiology that he will take cold without his blanket; whereas the wild animal, left to his instincts, sniffs the wind with delight." The connection of this quotation with what goes before shows that the horse does not take cold, in the opinion of Mrs. Eddy, because, having been accustomed to the blanket, his system is so weakened that he will take cold without it; but because the training of the said horse has been such that he is led to believe that if the blanket is not on he will take cold!

"CHRISTIAN SCIENCE" AND "MIND CURE"

they occur, as the sleeping victims of railroad disasters, are facts which, if they do not terminate human life at once, require the aid of surgery.

Mrs. Eddy says:

> The fear of dissevered bodily members, or a belief in such a possibility, is reflected on the body, in the shape of headache, fractured bones, dislocated joints, and so on, as directly as shame is seen in the blush rising to the cheek. This human error about physical wounds and colics is part and parcel of the delusion that matter can feel and see, having sensation and substance.

It is confessed, however, that very little progress has been made in this department:

> Christian Science is always the most skilful surgeon, but surgery is the branch of its healing that will be last demonstrated. However, it is but just to say that I have already in my possession well-authenticated records of the cure, by mental surgery alone, of dislocated hip-joints and spinal vertebrae.

But records, to be well authenticated, require more than an assertion. And the records may be authentic, and what they contain may never have been thoroughly tested. As they affirm that "bones have only the substance of thought, they are only an appearance to mortal mind"; if their theories be true at all, they should be able to rectify every result of accident to the body as readily and speedily as diseases originating within the system.

Fourth Test. Insanity. It is a well-established fact that blows upon the head produce insanity. It is equally well established that surgery in many cases is able to remove the difficulty by an obviously physical readjustment, where the surgeon himself cannot be positive what the effect will be until after the experiment, and the victim has no knowledge whatever upon the subject. During the late war, a negro was wounded in the head by the explosion of a shell. He wandered about for several years, to all appearance a driveling idiot, when certain surgeons took an interest in his case, and concluded that the removal of a piece of the skull which had been driven in and pressed upon the brain, might restore his reason. Knowing that no damage could be done to his mind by the operation, they performed it, and were almost appalled when, after the lapse of so many years, as they lifted the piece of skull and removed the pressure upon the brain, the light of intelligence returned to the eye of the man, who said, "We were at Manassas yesterday ; where are we to-day?" A similar case, where there had been delirium alternating with coma for a week, occurred in March last.

The transient effect of stimulants upon persons who have been in a state of dementia apparently for a long time, is also well known.

Mrs. Eddy upon this subject directs practitioners to tell the moderately sick man,

that he suffers only as the insane suffer, from a mere belief. The only difference is that insanity implies belief in a diseased brain, while physical ailments (so called) arise from belief that some other portions of the body are deranged. . . . The entire mortal body is evolved from mortal mind. A bunion would produce insanity as perceptible as that produced by congestion of the brain, were it not that mortal mind calls the bunion an unconscious portion of the body. Reverse this belief, and the results would be different.

It may be readily admitted that if a man believed his mind was in his foot, and believed it was out of order, he might be crazy. But in selecting the bunion for an illustration, Mrs. Eddy was not so wide of the mark as she might have been. More than twenty years ago, while listening to the lectures of Dr. C. E.

Brown-Séquard, before the physicians of Brooklyn, I heard him give the following case: A youth (fourteen years old) went to bed perfectly sane, nor had he ever had a symptom of insanity. The next morning when he arose and stepped upon the floor he became a maniac. With great difficulty he was replaced upon the bed, and the moment he touched it he was sane. During the morning he made several attempts to rise, always with the same result. A physician was called, who in his account of the case says: "When sitting up in his bed he drew on his stockings; but on *putting his feet on the floor and standing up, his countenance instantly changed, the jaw became violently convulsed,* etc. He was pushed back on the bed, was at once calm, looked surprised, and asked what was the matter. Inquiry showed that he had been fishing the preceding day, but had met with no accident. His legs were examined minutely, but nothing unusual was seen; but, says the physician, "*On holding up the right great toe with my finger and thumb to examine the sole of that foot, the leg was drawn up and the muscles of the jaws were suddenly convulsed, and on releasing the toe these effects instantly ceased.*" After further experiment, an irritated point, so small as to be scarcely visible, was taken away by the cutting of a piece of skin, and "the strange sensation was gone and never returned."[1]

---

[1] This case can be found (No. 44) in "Lectures on the Physiology and Pathology of the Central Nervous System," by Brown-Séquard; published, 1860, in Philadelphia. Also in Holmes's "Annals of Surgery," vol. 3, p. 330.

A similar account can be found of insanity produced four years after a boy trod on a piece of glass, which was entirely relieved by removing from a point near the ball of the big toe a trifling piece of glass. What is called the nervous temperament or condition is of importance.

Post-mortem examinations which exhibit the degeneration of the brain structure are of no importance in the eyes of these professors of dreams.

Fifth Test. The perpetuation of youth and the abolition of death should also be within the range of these magicians.

Baldwin, of Chicago, says:

> Man should grow younger as he grows older; the principle is simple. "As we think so are we" is stereotyped. Thoughts and ideas are ever striving for external expression. By keeping the mind young we have a perfect guarantee for continued youthfulness of body. Thought will externalize itself; thus growing thought will ever keep us young. Reliance on drugs makes the mind, consequently the body, prematurely old. This new system will make us younger at seventy than at seventeen, for then we will have more of genuine philosophy.

Mrs. Eddy meets this matter in the style of Jules Verne:

> The error of thinking that we are growing old, and the benefits of destroying that illusion, are illustrated in a sketch from the history of an English lady, published in the London "Lancet." Disappointed in love in early years she became insane. She lost all calculation of time. Believing that she still lived in the same hour that parted her from her lover, she took no note of years, but daily stood before the window, watching for his coming. In this mental state she remained young. Having no appearance of age, she literally grew no older. Some American travelers saw her when she was seventy-four, and supposed her a young lady. Not a wrinkle or gray hair appeared, but youth sat gently on cheek and brow. Asked to judge her age, and being unacquainted with her history, each visitor conjectured that she must be under twenty.

That the above should be adduced as proof of anything would be wonderful if the person adducing it had not previously adopted a theory which supersedes the necessity of demonstration. It is important to notice that if the belief had anything to do with it, this amazing result grew from a belief in a falsehood. She did *not* live in the same hour that parted her from her lover; she believed that she did, and, according to Mrs. Eddy, this belief of a falsehood counteracted all the ordinary consequences of the flight of time.

But the delusion among the insane that they are young, that they are independent of time and of this world, is very common; and the most painfully paradoxical sights that I have ever witnessed have been men and women, toothless, denuded of hair, and with all the signs of age,—sans teeth, sans eyes, sans taste, sans everything,—some of them declaring that they were young girls and engaged to be married to presidents and kings, and even to divine beings. These delusions in some instances have been fixed for many years. Having had an official connection with an insane asylum for five years, I have had more opportunities than were desired for conversing with persons of this class.

Granting the case adduced by Mrs. Eddy to be true, and admitting that the state of the mind may have had some effect, it is of no scientific importance; for the number who show no signs of age until fifty, sixty, or even seventy years have passed, is by no means small in the aggregate; we meet them everywhere. One of the most astute observers of human nature, himself a physician, solemnly warned a gentleman that if he continued to take only four hours' sleep in twenty-four, he would die before he was fifty years of age. "What do you suppose my age to be now?" said the gentleman. "Thirty," said the physician. "I am sixty-nine," was the reply, which proved to be the fact.

Mrs. Eddy, not content with this case, continues: "I have seen age regain two of the elements it had lost, sight and teeth. A lady of eighty-five whom I knew had a return of sight. Another lady at ninety had new teeth,—incisors, cuspids, bicuspids, and one molar." Such instances as these are not uncommon, but are generally a great surprise to the persons themselves, and unconnected with any delusion as to flight of time. They are simply freaks of nature.

There is a flattening of the eye which comes on with advancing years, and necessitates the use of glasses. Many persons who have few signs of age, retain the color of the cheek, have lost no teeth, and whose natural force is not abated, find their eyes dim. According to these metaphysical healers this is not necessary, but I have observed that a number of them say nothing about being themselves compelled to use glasses.

Much is made of one case of a metaphysical healer, who, after using glasses fifteen years, threw them away, and can now read even in the railroad cars without them. Such cases of second sight have occurred at intervals always, and under all systems, and sometimes when the progress of old age had been so great that the persons had suffered many infirmities, and had but a few months left in which to "see as well as ever they did in their lives."

Some famous actors and actresses, without the use of pigments, dyes, or paints, notwithstanding the irregular hours and other accidents of their professional life, have maintained an astonishing youthfulness of appearance down to nearly threescore years and ten.

John Wesley at seventy-five, according to testimony indubitable and from a variety of sources, not only presented the appearance of a man not yet past the prime of life, but, what is more remarkable, had the undiminished energy, vivacity, melody and strength of voice which accompany youth. Nor at eighty-five had he exhibited much change. In the city of Chicago there died recently a professional man nearly seventy-five years of age, whose teeth, complexion, color, hair, voice, and mind showed no signs of his being over forty-five years of age. Henry Ward Beecher, the January before his death, could write to his oldest brother that he had no rheumatism, neuralgia, sleeplessness, or deafness, was not bald, and did not need spectacles.

Meanwhile it is impossible not to suppose that the case as described by Mrs. Eddy has been greatly exaggerated. That some Americans who saw her at the age of seventy-four supposed her to be under twenty, is to be taken "*cum grano salis.*"

As for death, if the theories of these romantic philosophers be true, it should give way; if not in every case, at least in some. It is said that there are hundreds of persons in Boston who believe that Mrs. Eddy will never die. Joanna Southcott, who arose in England in 1792, made many disciples, by some estimated at one hundred thousand, who believed that she would never die; but unfortunately for their credulity she succumbed to the inevitable decree.

Sixth Test. If these theories are true, clothing, so far as sustaining warmth and life is concerned, is superfluous, and fire unnecessary. This conclusion reduces the whole scheme to an absurdity.

EXPLANATION OF THEIR ALLEGED SUCCESS

IN endeavoring to ascertain the causes of recoveries which undoubtedly occur when the patient is under the supervision of Christian Scientists and Mind Curers, it would be a blunder to omit the testimony of Mrs. Eddy as to her experiments with homeopathy. She says that she has attenuated common table salt until there was not a single saline property left; and yet with one drop of that in a goblet of water, and a teaspoonful administered every three hours, she has cured a patient sinking in the last stage of typhoid fever. Describing a case of dropsy given up by the faculty, she says that after giving some medicines of high attenuation, she gave the patient unmedicated pellets for a while, and found that she continued to improve. Finally she induced the patient to give up her medicine for one day, and risk the effects. After trying this, she informed Mrs. Eddy that she could get along two days without the globules; but on the third day had to take them. She went on in this way, taking unmedicated pellets, with occasional visits from Mrs. Eddy, and employing no other means was cured. Thus Mrs. Eddy says she discovered that mind was potent over matter and that drugs have no power.

It is not to be inferred from the above that homeopathic remedies, which have been modified by the discoveries made and the experience attained since the time of Hahnemann, are generally powerless. That question is not essential to this inquiry. But the confession of Mrs. Eddy that her experiments were the means of teaching her that mind and not matter effects the cure, will be regarded by all who do not accept her theories as containing the principal key to the problem. She made the common error of generalizing from a few particulars, and ever since has endeavored to test facts by theory instead of making facts the test. Because she found a supposed mental cause adequate to a cure in a few cases, she leaped to the wild conclusion that all causes are mental. Notwithstanding these numerous absurdities and the radical error, it would be unwise to lose sight of the specific elements in the practice of Christian Science and the various forms of Mind Cure as a profession.

The patients who are treated by these practitioners have, to begin with, the *vis medicatrix naturæ*, which is the final element in every cure, recognized to be such by the leaders of the medical profession for a long period of time. Sir John Forbes, M. D., one of the most eminent regular physicians of England, remarks of the practice of his own School in his famous article on homeopathy:

> First, that in a large proportion of the cases treated by allopathic physicians, the disease is cured by nature, and not by them. Second, that in a lesser but still not a small proportion, the disease is cured by nature in spite of them; in other words, their interference retarding instead of assisting the cure. Third, that in, consequently, a considerable proportion of diseases it would fare as well or better with patients if all remedies — at least all active remedies, especially drugs — were abandoned.

Sydenham long ago said, "I often think more could be left to Nature than we are in the habit of leaving to her; to imagine that she always wants the help of art is an error, and an unlearned error too."

Sir John Marshall, F. R. S., in opening the session of the London University Medical School in 1865, said,

> The *vis medicatrix naturæ* is the agent to employ in the healing of an ulcer, or the union of a broken bone; and it is equally true that the physician or surgeon never cured a disease; he only assists the natural processes of cure performed by the intrinsic conservative energy of the frame, and this is but the extension of the force imparted at the origination of the individual being.

Under the Mind Cure this force of nature is still at work, and in the great number of self-limited diseases which tend to recovery, it is left free from all error of practitioners. If it loses any advantages which the introduction of the proper drugs might give, it is saved from the consequences of the administration of the wrong ones.

The number of instances in which the prescriptions interfere with nature is so great that Dr. Paris wrote, many years ago, "The file of every apothecary would furnish a volume of instances where the ingredients of the prescription were fighting together in the dark. This is especially true of diseases of children. The late Dr. Marshall Hall said, "Of the whole number of fatal cases of diseases in infancy, a great proportion occur from the inappropriate or undue application of exhausting remedies."

Further, those who are treated by the Mind Curers in many cases derive benefit from the freedom of diet, air, and exercise allowed. They are told to pay no attention to symptoms, think nothing whatever about their diseases, and not talk about them; to eat, sleep, drink, and act as nearly as possible as if they were well; and in a large majority of chronic diseases, this is all that is needed to produce a return to health.

They have also the benefits of faith and fancy; as they are taught to imagine healthy, vigorous organs, and their whole bodies in the condition of health, and with such mental pictures to drive away all consciousness of symptoms, they summon to their aid that most potent of all influences, a calm and fearless mind. The presence of the practitioner and her methods greatly contribute to this calming influence.

> She enters with a cheerful air and, without taking your hand or approaching your bed, seats herself and asks you to tell her all your symptoms. [She may, however, belong to the class which will not allow any description of symptoms.] She receives your budget of ailments calmly, without one expression of sympathy, for she has none, considering all your maladies as an illusion or dream from which it is her divine mission to

"CHRISTIAN SCIENCE" AND "MIND CURE"

awaken you. You are made to feel, immediately, that there is little of consequence in all that you have been telling her. She then relapses into a silence of ten or fifteen minutes, in which her kind face wears a resolute expression, making it almost stern. . . . After this silent treatment she speaks to you in the most encouraging manner, endeavoring to call you away from yourself to the contemplation of spiritual truth.

A point of difference between Faith Healers and Mind Curers is worthy of observation. Faith Healers require the patient to have faith; Mind Curers make a boast of the fact that faith is not necessary. A close analysis, however, shows that this boast is vain. Before they are sent for there is usually some faith, and often much, combined with a distrust of other systems. This was, as some of their authorities affirm, the case when they began. Sufficient time has elapsed to develop a constituency who employ no other methods. If there is no faith, there must be a distrust of other forms of practice, or there would be no reason for turning to the new. Where there is no faith on the part of the patient, usually his friends believe, and have induced him to make the experiment. Thus he is surrounded by an atmosphere of faith which is so important that all the writers attach great weight to it.

> Friends and attendants who are believers in Mental cure, and know what sort of a mental atmosphere is favorable to restoring health, may do much to help the metaphysician in his work. But, unfortunately, this is seldom the case; and the friends are usually ignorant on the subject, and innocently burdening the invalid with just that kind of hurtful sympathy which keeps him under a cloud of depression. When such is the case, their absence is more helpful than their presence, and it is desirable to be alone with the patient while treating him.—MARSTON.

Some even go so far as to say that they should be, if possible, removed from the society of those who do not believe.

But a favorable atmosphere exists to some extent among those who have induced an unbelieving invalid to send for a mental healer. Assuming that the healer has arrived, it is easy to see how faith is engendered. She takes her seat, and after a few unimportant questions becomes silent. The thoughts that wander through the mind of the invalid, as told me by a patient of thorough intelligence, an alumnus of one of the first universities of this country, were such as these: "Can there be anything in this? I don't believe there is, and yet a great many people are believing in it, and some most wonderful cures have taken place. There is Mrs. ——. I *know* that she was given up to die by our best physicians, and I *know* that she is well." Then the eye will turn to the face of the metaphysician, who seems looking at far-off things and wrestling with some problem not yet solved, but of the certainty of the solution of which she has no doubt. Sometimes the practitioners cover their eyes, and this would add to the effect in many temperaments. The fifteen minutes pass and leave the unbeliever passive; as a quotation elsewhere describes it, "less cantankerous."

The encouraging words of the healer on departing are not without effect, differing as they do from the uncertain or preternaturally solemn forthgivings, or ill-concealed misgivings, of many ordinary physicians. There are no medicines to take, no symptoms to watch, and only the certainty of recovery to be dwelt upon. Whatever the appetite calls for is to be eaten without anxiety as to the consequences, and if there be no appetite there is to be no eating and no anxiety as to the result of abstinence.

The effect of the treatment having been pleasant, the patient rather longs than otherwise for the next day to come, and for the next. If the disease be one

"CHRISTIAN SCIENCE" AND "MIND CURE"

that under ordinary circumstances would require an operation, the dreadful image of the surgeon's knife no longer appals the patient's mind. The invalid discovers that he does not die, that he sleeps a little better; certainly he is not aroused to take medicine, and there is no fear that he will take cold; he feels decidedly better at the next visit, and now faith is not only born but turned into sight. His friends assure him that he is better, and he tells them that he is so.

Perhaps the most potent cause in awakening faith is the sublime audacity displayed by the practitioner who dares to dispense with drugs, manipulation, hygiene, prayer, and religious ceremony. That spectacle would infallibly produce either such opposition and contempt as would result in the termination of the experiment, or faith. It is impossible to be in a negative position in its presence, where the responsibilities of life and death are assumed.

As for "absent treatments," these are based on the theory that to think of another entirely and abstractedly occasions a spiritual presence of that other. "Distance is annihilated, and his living image and inner personality seem to stand before us, and what we say to it we say to him."

These persons catch up and incorporate with their theories the yet immature investigations of the Society for Psychical Research, in which it is claimed that a sensitive subject can form in the mind a distinct mental picture or idea of words and letters which had been in the mind of an agent. Healers endeavor to extend those phenomena so as to make them annihilate space; and, according to them, "it is as easy to affect a person in the interior of Africa by a mental influence, as in the same room." Here they affiliate with the whole mass of superstitions which accumulated in the early history of the human race, and reappear in certain temperaments in each generation. Whether such a thing as thought-transference exists, there is not space here to inquire; nor is it necessary, for the effects of the "absent treatment," so called, can all be accounted for without any such assumption.

Patients thus treated *know* or they do *not* know that they are being treated. When they know, there is nothing to explain, for it is the same as if patient and practitioner were in each other's presence. All the mental operations, as well as the original force of nature, proceed under the conviction that they are being treated by a mental healer. If they do not know the entire field of coincidence and the *vis medicatrix naturæ* remain inviolate; and to determine that there is any connection between the alleged treatment and the change in the condition of the patient would require a vast number of cases and detailed coincidence of time and symptom, for which these practitioners do not display ability, and for which, on their own testimony, they have had no opportunity. Indeed, their theories are such as to make all investigation superfluous and tedious.

The case upon which Mrs. Eddy appears to rely is described thus: "The day you received my husband's letter I became conscious for the first time in forty-eight hours." What can this prove? What evidence is there that she would not have become conscious if the letter had never been written? If she were ever to come out of an unconscious state and recover, it must be at some time. The coincidence of Mrs. Eddy's receiving a letter from the husband does not show any connection between the two facts, for such letters have been sent and the patients have died. To my personal knowledge her treatments have failed, and her predictions have not been fulfilled, the patient dying in excruciating agony. Instances which have occurred, and can be reproduced at any time, of the attempted absent treatment of persons *who never existed*, are numerous; for there is not one of this class of healers that cannot be so imposed upon. This is sufficient to raise a powerful presumption that the spiritual presence which they evoke, and to which they speak, is "such stuff as dreams are made of."

It is not to be denied that they make more cures than any bungler or extremist of a school using drugs would expect. But their failures are numerous, and, like faith healers, they never publish *these*. Compelled, however, to admit this, the chancellor of the University of the Science of Spirit says:

> Our inability to heal instantaneously as they (Jesus and the Apostles) are recorded to have done, is attributable to our deficiency in the realization of the doctrine. While we claim that our theory of healing is applicable to all diseases, we do not claim to possess sufficient understanding in it at the present time to heal all diseases instantaneously, neither would we now guarantee to cure certain diseases, such as cancer or consumption in the last stages. Of one thing, however, we are confident, *i. e.*, that we can do more good in all cases of illness than can be done with any other theory, or with materia medica.—ARENS.

They are rather more successful than faith healers for this reason: with the faith healers it is generally either an instantaneous cure, or none at all. And an instantaneous cure cannot be made to apply to a great many cases, and what is supposed to be such is very frequently a delusion followed by a complete relapse. The Christian Scientists, however, and their congeners make many visits and give nature a much better opportunity without the destruction of the patient's faith in them by a failure at a critical juncture; thus it happens that the proportion of recoveries is more numerous.

The principal practical element has been more or less recognized and employed by the greatest physicians of every school through the whole history of medical practice, as well as by quacks and superstitious pagan priests. "The History of Medical Economy during the Middle Ages," by George F. Fort, contains numerous illustrations of this subject, though adduced for another purpose, and, unlike many other treatises, giving the authorities with most painstaking accuracy.

Dr. Rush, of whom Dr. Tuke affirms that few physicians have had more practical experience of disease, says:

> I have frequently prescribed remedies of doubtful efficacy in the critical stage of acute diseases, but never till I had worked up my patients into a confidence bordering upon certainty of their probable good effects. The success of this measure has much oftener answered than disappointed my expectations.

The "British and Foreign Medical Review" for January, 1846, whose editor then was Sir John Forbes, contained an article written by himself which encourages "the administration of simple, feeble, and altogether powerless, non-perturbing medicines, in all cases in which drugs are prescribed *pro forma*, for the satisfaction of the patient's mind, and not with the view of producing any direct remedial effect."

"Physic and Physicians," published in 1839, speaking of the celebrated and extraordinarily successful Dr. Radcliffe, who was the founder of the Radcliffe Library at Oxford University, and died in 1714, says that he paid particular attention to the mind of the patient under his care, and had been heard to say that he attributed much of his success and eminence

"CHRISTIAN SCIENCE" AND "MIND CURE"

to this circumstance. There is a very good anecdote illustrating his views upon this subject:

> A lady of rank consulted Radcliffe in great distress about her daughter, and the doctor began the investigation of the case by asking, "Why, what ails her?" "Alas! doctor," replied the mother, "I cannot tell; but she has lost her humor, her looks, her stomach; her strength consumes every day, and we are apprehensive that she cannot live." "Why do you not marry her?" said Radcliffe. "Alas! doctor, that we would fain do, and have offered her as good a match as ever she could expect." "Is there no other that you think she would be content to marry?" "Ah, doctor, that is what troubles us; for there is a young gentleman we doubt she loves, that her father and I can never consent to." "Why, look you, madam," replied Radcliffe gravely, "then the case is this: your daughter would marry one man, and you would have her marry another. In all my books I find no remedy for such a disease as this."

This principle has also been employed by certain priests and clergymen of every sect. A young woman, a teacher, was, as she believed and as her friends supposed, at the point of death. Her physician was not quite certain that she was as ill as she seemed, and requested the pastor to assist him in breaking up her delusion that she must die. He attempted it, but she refused to hear him, and intrusted him with messages for her friends, especially for her class in the Sunday School. When about to bid her farewell, he informed her that he would return in the afternoon; she replied that she would like him to pray with her, but that it was useless to ask for her recovery. Having in view her hearing what he had to say, he prayed in such a way as to break the spell and cause her to believe that she would recover; as he did this, the morbid symptoms of approaching death gave way, and she is still living.

Another case was still more remarkable. A woman, ill and bedridden, conceived a high regard for the piety and intelligence of her pastor. He entered her room and in a loud and solemn voice said, "I command you to arise!" Involuntarily she arose and resumed the duties of housekeeping, which after the lapse of ten years she still performs.

A Roman Catholic priest, of high position in his church, told the writer that he thought he had saved scores of lives by refusing to administer the Sacrament of Extreme Unction, which led the patients to say "Father —— does not think I am going to die."

In 1832, when the cholera raged in Norfolk, Virginia, Dr. Buzzell, a physician of great local celebrity, lived there. He was driving night and day, and on one occasion was summoned to see a stalwart negro who was apparently in the state of collapse. Instead of beginning at once to treat him, he accused him of shamming, denounced and derided him in every possible way for calling him when he was at work night and day, driven almost to death. Then, assuming the appearance of intense excitement, he procured a switch and began to thrash the negro very severely. The more he groaned, and the more he said he was dying, the more Dr. Buzzell thrashed him, and with his threatenings and beatings brought on such a tremendous reaction that the man recovered.

In a visit to a branch of the Oneida Community at Wallingford, in 1856, I asked Mrs. Miller, the sister of John H. Noyes, the founder of the community, what they did if any of the inmates became ill, as they repudiated medicines. She said they had very little sickness. "But, have I not heard of an epidemic of diphtheria among you?" She said there had been, but by their treatment they saved every case. "What was that treatment?" "It was treatment by criticism." "How was it applied?" "So soon as a person was taken ill, a committee was appointed who went into the room and sat down, paying no attention to the patient; they began at once to speak about him or her, criticizing the patient's peculiarities, bringing every defect to the surface, and unsparingly condemning it." Mrs. Miller added that no one could endure this more than an hour. The mental and moral irritation was so great that they began to perspire and invariably recovered. The universal efficacy of this method may well be doubted, for many persons live in such an atmosphere that if that treatment would save them, they would never die; while others are so callous to all criticism that the remedy would be without effect.

In a certain lunatic asylum was a patient, a very attractive young lady, whose delusion took the form that she was specially called of God to do some great work which had not yet been indicated to her. With this were connected several pernicious practices, such as fasting, excessive prayer, and others of similar character. The asylum physicians were very much interested in her, but the months passed away and she did not improve.

At last one of the assistant physicians, especially interested in the influence of the mind upon the body, determined upon a plan to effect her cure by a powerful mental operation. Accordingly, he introduced a tube into her room, without her knowledge, and also prepared a calcium light so that, at a certain time, he could flood the room with rays of intense brilliancy.

The young woman had not walked a step for many months. At the appointed hour, with all the physicians standing in the hall, and the wife of the physician in chief—a thoroughly Christian woman, intensely sympathetic with the patient—also with them, the physician spoke through the tube in the name of the Lord, informing the girl that He had heard her prayers, that she should soon be sent upon her mission, and that she should go forth from the place to her own home to testify to His glory. At the same instant that the voice was heard, the room was flooded with a light much brighter than the sun at noonday.

Her face, with the utmost simplicity of faith, was lighted up with a joy that seemed too great for mortal; and those who were situated where they could see it, declared that hardly ever in their lives had they seen such an expression of seraphic bliss.

Of course, great interest centered in the conduct of the young woman the next morning. She said not a word to a human being upon her vision, but in the morning rose and walked the entire length of the hall, and continued to improve in physical and mental health till discharged from the asylum as practically cured.

Our informant, an official of the institution, of entire credibility, has not heard from her for some time; but, up to a recent period, she remained in good health.

This is an instance of cure effected by the operation of the mind upon the body, as extraordinary as any instance of cure which can be adduced by Faith Healers or Christian Scientists.

The nervous "temperament" or condition of the healer appears to be of no special importance; that is, it is of importance only in the same sense that it is to salesmen, public speakers, school-teachers, lawyers, sea-captains, detectives, military leaders, physicians, and all who impress themselves upon others. I have seen successful healers thin and tall; others short and fat; some pale, others florid; some intelligent, others unintelligent; some intellectual, more only intelligent; some in good health, others diseased; one of the best was so feeble as to seem on the verge of death.[1]

The specimen mental treatment given on page 257 shows how the practitioner worked herself up to the point; and it is easy to fancy how forcibly she spoke when a surge of conviction that seemed to act on all the blood-vessels of her body and made her tingle all over, went through her; and it is equally easy to imagine the effect upon the patient.

The relation of the Mind Cure movement to ordinary medical practice is important. It emphasizes what the most philosophical physicians of all schools have always deemed of the first importance, though many have neglected it. It teaches that medicine is but occasionally necessary. It hastens the time when patients of discrimination will rather pay more for advice how to live, and for frank declarations that they do not need medicine, than for drugs. It promotes general reliance upon those processes which go on equally in health and disease.

But these ethereal practitioners have no new force to offer; there is no causal connection between their cures and their theories.

What they believe has practically nothing to do with their success. If a new school were to arise

---

[1] In practice it seems to be more difficult to successfully treat one's self than to treat another person. The reason for this is that, when personally under the influence of supposed disease, the appeal of the senses is more forcible than when the deception shows itself in another. But that one can conquer the results of his own inverted thinking, there is not the slightest occasion to doubt. . . . We must not, however, make the mistake of supposing that he who would attempt to bring healing to others must first be sound himself. . . . The effect of a treatment depends not on its length, but on the condition of the healer who exercises it, and the dynamic power of the thought exerted.—MARSTON.

claiming to heal diseases without drugs or hygiene, or prayer, by the hypothetical odylic force invented by Baron Reichenbach, the effects would be the same, if the practice were the same.

Recoveries as remarkable have been occurring through all the ages, as the results of mental states and nature's own powers.

They will not be able to displace either the skilled surgeon or the educated physician; for their arrogant and exclusive pretensions are of the nature of a "craze." Most sensible persons will prefer a physician who understands both the mind and the body; who can be a "father confessor" to the sick man, relieving him of the responsibility of treating himself, quieting his mind, strengthening him by hope, and stimulating him by his personal presence; one who, understanding the mineral, plant, and animal substances included in the materia medica, can assist nature, interfering only when absolutely necessary and certainly safe; too learned and honest, when not knowing what to do, ever to do he knows not what.

They will also prefer a physician who can relieve their pains when incurable, smooth their pathway to the inevitable end, or, when he has the happiness to see them convalescent, will be able to give them such hygienic hints as may prevent a recurrence of the malady, or save them from something worse.

The verdict of mankind, excepting minds prone to vagaries on the borderland of insanity, will be that pronounced by Ecclesiasticus more than two thousand years ago:

"THE LORD HATH CREATED MEDICINES OUT OF THE EARTH; AND HE THAT IS WISE WILL NOT ABHOR THEM. MY SON, IN THY SICKNESS BE NOT NEGLIGENT; BUT PRAY UNTO THE LORD, AND HE WILL MAKE THEE WHOLE. LEAVE OFF FROM SIN, AND ORDER THY HANDS aright, and cleanse thy heart from all wickedness. Then give place to the physician, for the Lord hath created him: let him not go from thee, for thou hast need of him. There is a time when in their hands there is good success. For they shall also pray unto the Lord, that he would prosper that which they give for ease and to prolong life."

SUPPLEMENTARY PAPER

RECENT FAILURES OF CHRISTIAN SCIENCE AND FAITH HEALING

FOR some time after Christian Science arose, the number of believers being comparatively small, there were not many deaths; and, except among aged persons or during an epidemic of some unusually fatal malady, there is never a large relative proportion of deaths among adults in any period of a few years. The life-table for England and Wales (Supplement to Fifty-fifth Annual Report of the Registrar-General, 1895) states that of one million persons born, 737,617 live to the age of seventeen, and 427,497 to the age of sixty. This table was based on the mortality of the ten years 1881-90.

Nineteen years ago I collected vital statistics of various communistic institutions, and of small cities and towns, and on the basis of the results of the experiments I predicted that, should Christian Science at any time begin to spread rapidly, or should anti-medicine Faith Healing institutions be largely increased, the number of deaths would attract public attention, and indignation would be excited by failures to heal maladies which ordinarily yield to medical or surgical treatment. This has come to pass, and scarcely a paper can be taken up which does not contain an account of persons dying, often in great agony, who have not been attended by any one who has devoted his life to the acquisition of knowledge of the human system, the action of remedies, and the most skilful methods of imparting the aid which science can give.

A large correspondence, stimulated by the publication of these articles, leads me to conclude that but a small proportion of such deaths comes to the notice of the public. Only occasionally, when physicians refuse to sign a certificate of death,— in many parts of the country this is frequently neglected,— is attention directed to it. Friends of the deceased are often so ashamed of having adopted a view which in the estimation of minds well informed and well balanced is absurd, that they remain silent. Several such instances have been communicated to me in confidence.

Christian Scientists and Faith Healers make great efforts to keep unbelievers from the sick-room, in the former case upon the theory that they prevent the patient's understanding the principles which are sufficient to drive sickness away, and in the latter that they prevent the patient from exercising faith; hence it is difficult to obtain legal evidence of what is actually done, and of the state of the patient at any particular time. The assertion is often made that "in any case the patient would have died," and medical men can readily be found to plaster the scandal with a certificate. Instances have occurred of summoning a physician and securing a prescription in order to be able to say that one was called, and then refusing to administer the medicine.

CONTRAST BETWEEN THE FAILURES AND SUCCESSES OF FAITH HEALING AND CHRISTIAN SCIENCE AND THOSE OF PHYSICIANS

CHRISTIAN SCIENTISTS and Faith Healers agree in protesting against the publication of their failures, alleging that if those of the medical profession were likewise exploited its members would be more effectually discredited than are they.

This protest seems plausible, but will not bear examination. Christian Scientists boast of millions of cures of diseases ordinarily incurable. In the brief period of a fortnight a noted lecturer changed the sum total from "one million" to "millions." The followers of Mrs. Eddy deny the existence of disease; the followers of Dowie in the West and of Simpson in the East claim that the power of Christ is exercised in answer to their prayers. Dowie rivals the Christian Scientist lecturers in boasting, and Simpson makes claims of recoveries little less miraculous than would be the raising of the dead. Their failures are incompatible with their main contention.

In contrast with these self-deceivers and deceivers of others the physician knows that all men must die, and that all die of old age, disease, accident, or intentional violence. He claims by hygiene, medicine, and surgery to assist nature in the struggle to delay the inevitable and render the progress to it more endurable. If he has qualified himself by the acquisition of all available learning and skill, whether the patients perfectly recover or but partly recover, whether, indeed, the patient live or die, the physician if unworthy is amenable only to the charge of neglect or malpractice.

But Christian Scientists contemptuously reject all the knowledge the human race has secured, exclude from the sick-room those who possess it, deny that remedies have any power, and cannot consistently use opiate or anesthetic, the greatest boon which science has conferred on man. Their anodyne for the agony that finds expression in the heartrending cry is the reiteration, "There is no disease," "There is no pain," "Think only of God, not as person but as principle." Faith Healers turn from what God has endued with healing virtues, from what even the instincts of animals, when ill, prompt them to seek, lest the use of means should prevent the exercise of the power of God! Those who promise and attempt so much while rejecting so much cannot consistently ask indulgence.

When a physician or surgeon is guilty of neglect or malpractice, the victim, or in case of death his "next of kin," or, should these decline to demand an investigation, the authorities, can summon the accused physician to trial, and the case may be equitably decided upon what he has done or has neglected to do; but if he has been under the care of Christian Scientists or Faith Healers all that might have been done was intentionally neglected.

IMPORTANT FACTS CONCERNING ALL SICKNESSES

THAT many sick persons would recover without treatment of any kind is certain. That many who would not recover without encouragement will do so where confidence is inspired and maintained has often been demonstrated. Christian Scientists, Faith Healers, Mind Curers, the venders of pads and bogus electrical apparatus, of alleged magical rings, and other forms of deception, and also skilful physicians, receive the benefit of all such cases, and adduce them to persuade the people to accept their claims and services. That many who are hypochondriacal and hysterical would be well if they could be made to think they are, and to act accordingly, is beyond doubt. All classes of practitioners, and the votaries of all religions, true and false, receive the benefit of such recoveries, the cure being wrought by the vital force which preserves the body from birth till death.

But there are diseases, and particular instances of almost every trifling disease, which will not terminate if left to themselves. There are many injuries which, without external aid, nature never did and never can repair. There are conditions so painful that, though the disease would not destroy life, the pain will surely overthrow reason or cause death, unless the sense of it can be deadened.

Science has discovered in nature simples, or ascertained how to form compounds, which, properly administered, will, by removing obstructions which increase or diminish the flow of blood, assist nature to restore health. In a multitude of cases where the vital force contends with the influence of poisons, either externally administered or engendered within the body, or where vital organs are deranged or obstructed, or the patient is in such a mental condition that Christian Scientists and Faith Healers could render no encouragement and receive no coöperation, science working in harmony with chemical laws and animal life, and, when necessary, by the mechanical art of surgery, can and does succeed. In any case where nature unaided is plainly competent to throw off the incubus, whatever its cause, learned and skilful physicians will give only that which alleviates the pain of symptoms, and will depend upon natural force, hygiene, and encouragement.

Minds so constituted as to accept either Christian Science or anti-medicine Faith Healing can listen unmoved to the groans of the sufferer, and by constant incantations of words encourage him to hold on and not "betray the cause." Christian Scientists can declare that dreadful symptoms are only "chemicalization."[1] Faith Healers can charge their followers

[1] See page 79.

with want of faith, threaten them with damnation and incite them to almost superhuman efforts to believe. In case of failure, these are not slow to intimate that the deceased or the incurable yielded to temptation of the devil, and fell into unbelief.

Indians in their wildest dances cannot become more insensible to the pain of others or themselves than do some of the intellectual fanatics of the present day. In this city, a woman about to become a mother, believing fully in one of these delusions, sent for some of its advocates. Hour after hour her pangs increased until they became intolerable, and she exclaimed, "Send for a physician!" With one accord they adjured her not to "betray the cause." For twelve hours she shrieked in agony. The neighbors heard and threatened to summon the police. A physician was called. The room was vacated by all except the nurse and the physician. In five minutes, by means of a harmless anesthetic, her pains became endurable, and after some hours of constant work the danger point was passed. Then the physician summoned those fanatics, and told them to give thanks to God that they had been prevented from committing a double murder.

So completely under the dominion of their respective fetishes are many that neither death nor failure to cure depresses them in the least degree.

While Christian Science and anti-medicine Faith Healing are alike responsible for many deaths and for suffering that might have been prevented, the former has been the indirect, and in some cases the direct, cause of a number of cases of insanity. If the theory of Christian Science be true, the use of food should be unnecessary. Total abstinence from food beyond a limited period produces a universal disease popularly known as starvation, and also diseases of particular organs, and other maladies, the result of the want of force for the performance of the various excretory and other functions of the system, the sure end of which is death. If the theory of Christian Science be true, the same methods which cause disease originating in other ways to disappear should be adequate to counterwork the effects of the non-use of food. I have met several instances of Christian Scientists who have carried the matter to the length of refusing to eat. If it be assumed that such must have been insane before going to such an extreme, this would go far toward proving want of balance in the mind that could accept fundamental propositions from which this course is a logical consequence. In one family a brother and two sisters recently became demented, and were removed to institutions for the insane.

THE RELATION OF THE PRACTICE OF CHRISTIAN SCIENCE AND FAITH HEALING TO CIVIL LAW

THE relation of this subject to civil law is beginning to attract the attention proportionate to its importance. Physicians have been slow to move, lest they should be charged with selfish motives, and the clergy have been comparatively silent concerning legal restraints, lest they should seem to wish to interfere with rights of conscience.

The theory of this government is based upon the largest degree of individual freedom compatible with the welfare of society. These eccentrics claim that non-use of medicine is a part of their religion. So the Mormons claimed that polygamy was a part of their religion. Religious freedom implies the right to think what one pleases; but this cannot justify the violation of laws not made for the suppression of religion, but for the protection of the community. Hence the suppression of polygamy received the approbation of all classes excepting those who practised it.

In the application of legal restraint the law forbids the practice of healing by any not duly licensed upon examination before a competent and legally established board. The mere fact that persons do not prescribe medicine is not sufficient to prove that they are not in a proper sense of the term medical practitioners. Hydropathists, depending entirely upon the internal and external use of water, together with friction, are medical practitioners. Those who for pay give to invalids counsel with regard to health, whether they prescribe medicine or not, are medical practitioners. No one can compel, and no law should be made to require, a sane adult, not suffering from a contagious disease, to take medicine if he does not wish to do so, even though the presumption be that he might derive benefit from treatment, and will die prematurely if he does not submit to it. But should an adult, the victim of an acute or chronic disease, sink into coma or become delirious, he is then a proper subject for interference, if those in charge of him refuse to call medical or surgical aid; for irresponsible beings are the wards of the State.

Instances have occurred in which the adult while sane called for medical aid; but on his becoming delirious his relatives have discharged the physician and summoned Christian Scientists or anti-medicine Faith Healers. It is self-evident that when it is shown that a patient receiving no treatment has become unconscious or delirious, the law is justified in interfering.

Children also are the wards of the State, and are

left to the care of parents when there is no reason to believe them unfaithful to the trust, or incompetent to fulfil it. If credible witnesses testify to neglect or incompetence, the State is justified in interfering. Therefore if parents refuse their children medical treatment when suffering from any disease which might prove fatal, the State is justified at least in requiring the attendance of health-officers, and if they believe the situation critical, in enforcing treatment.

If the disease be contagious the State should take charge of the patient, and require that he be treated by those methods which the civilization of the age approves, and this not only for the sake of the sufferer, but of the thousands who are liable to contract the malady if it is not promptly cured or isolated. Compulsory vaccination is an illustration of the same principle, and since many contagious diseases are distinguishable only by expert physicians when there is any reason to suspect their existence, their management should not be left to those who on principle attach no importance to the knowledge of the nature of any disease, their methods being the same whether it is a case of smallpox, the bubonic plague, leprosy, scarlet fever, diphtheria, or a simple cold.

To check the tide of public indignation certain prominent practitioners of Christian Science are credited to have said that, "if in four or five hours" they "produce no impression upon any one who thinks that he is ill," they "are in the habit of recommending that a physician be sent for." If this be true, the confession of weakness and inconsistency is pitiable, and why should the law allow persons neither qualified nor licensed, whose theory requires them to ignore and to teach patients to ignore symptoms, to decide when a physician should be called. Others have avowed that they "take no fees," accepting only what the patient freely gives. This is analogous to the course of those legislators who "take no bribes," but "receive only the free gifts of personal friends." In the eyes of the law they are "medical practitioners" if in the habit of responding to calls for treatment.

Where laws sufficient to deal with such cases as these do not exist, they should be enacted, and where they already exist, be strictly enforced. The sane adult can then pursue his way, the cry of persecution will have no foundation, and the religious cults with which these delusions are connected will increase or decline in proportion to their adaptation to the religious needs of mankind.

www.ingramcontent.com/pod-product-compliance
Lightning Source LLC
Chambersburg PA
CBHW020100170426
43199CB00009B/349